Music and Society

The last post

Music and Society

Series editor Peter Martin

Further titles are in preparation

Edited by
Simon Miller

The last post
Music after modernism

Manchester University Press
Manchester and New York

Distributed exclusively in the USA and Canada by St. Martin's Press

Published by Manchester University Press
Oxford Road, Manchester M13 9PL, UK
and Room 400, 175 Fifth Avenue,
New York, NY 10010, USA

Distributed exclusively in the USA and Canada
by St. Martin's Press, Inc.,
175 Fifth Avenue, New York, NY 10010, USA

British Library cataloguing in publication data

A catalogue record for this book is available from the British Library

Library of Congress cataloging in publication data applied for

ISBN 0 7190 3609 7 *hardback*

Typeset in Hong Kong
by Best-Set Typesetter Ltd, Hong Kong

Printed in Great Britain
by Biddles Ltd, Guildford and King's Lynn

Contents

Acknowledgements

This book has been some time coming to fruition. My thanks to all those who have helped me and the other contributors with its completion. To my first editor, John Banks, whose encouragement got the project off the ground. To Jo Travis and Anita Roy, his successors at MUP, and Dr Peter Martin of Manchester University who have so patiently seen the work into publication.

Dr Carolyn Brown and Professor Simon Frith provided many helpful suggestions and Sara Haworth offered support in the initial stages.

Finally, I express my gratitude to Lindsey Shaw – the editor's editor. Her love, companionship and acuity are deeply felt. My thanks to her also for compiling the index. I dedicate this work to her and to my parents Olive and Tom.

Simon Miller

Simon Miller

Introduction

The idea for this book came from developments which have taken place in the field of art history. My own work has for a number of years focused on the relationships between the visual arts and music, and it is through contact with so called 'new art history' methodologies that I became aware of the difference in the approach to the study of the 'object' in these two disciplines. The term 'new art history' needs some definition. As Rees and Borzello write in their introduction to *The New Art History*:

Rather than a tidy description of one trend, the new art history is a capacious and convenient title that sums up the impact of feminist, marxist, structuralist, psychoanalytic, and social-political ideas on a discipline notorious for its conservative taste in art and its orthodoxy in research.[1]

Until very recently the study of music has been perhaps even more 'conservative and orthodox' in its approach. This can be seen in part in the distinction that is made between musicology and music history, separating formal questions from contextual ones. We can paraphrase Roskill from his book *What is Art History?* (1974), in his description of the traditional approach to the study of the discipline, and apply it to the study of music. In this way study has most often proceeded with questions of 'style, attributions, dating, authenticity, rarity, reconstruction, the detection of forgery, the rediscovery of forgotten artists [musicians/composers] and the meanings of pictures [pieces of music]'. This last point is perhaps more problematic in the case of music, given its 'abstract' nature, and is an issue I shall discuss in Chapter 1. Such a 'conservative' approach was challenged within art history by T. J.

Clark's call, in 1972 (*The Times Literary Supplement*), for a study of
the discipline which took account of the realities of the social world
in which art is produced. In adopting a similar approach in relation
to music, I am not suggesting that traditional approaches to the
study of the subject are wrong, just that they do not ask, or are
incapable of asking, a number of important and difficult questions.
Such issues have even more relevance given the discussions which
surround the concept of postmodernism. This idea has given rise
to more overt considerations of contextual issues, which tend
to challenge the predominantly formalist concerns of modernist
criticism. However, the term *postmodernism* has been given widely
disparate meanings by a number of authors, as is evident in the
present collection. It might therefore be useful if I make clear, in
brief, my own position in regard to this increasingly popular buzz-
word.

Firstly, I do not regard the 'postmodern condition' as culturally
(or for that matter politically) all-embracing, affecting all people,
destroying all meta-narratives, breaking down all cultural polarities
(high/low distinctions); rather I would argue it relates to a problematic aspect of the 'contemporary condition'. It helps to frame, in
other words, our difficulty in anchoring meaning within clear
boundaries.

Secondly, I do not therefore regard the most significant question
as just one of meaning but rather one of the relationships of
meaning to questions of power and authority. Finally, I regard postmodernism as a crisis in the culture of modernism and modernisation rather than a complete rupture with it, one which maintains
and appropriates aspects of modernist strategies in the process of
recontextualising them.

It is particularly important to engage with these questions
in relation to music-making, precisely because music has been
privileged as an unproblematised paradigm, within conventional
musicology; a socially and politically autonomous art (see Chapter
1). To disrupt this *telos*, to make apparent the contradictions of this
project, particularly within the complex of contemporary capitalist
life, is thus, I believe, politically crucial. This could take the form
of a postmodernism of resistance; a recognition or celebration of
diversity and difference ('otherness'), as they emerge in subjectivity,
gender, sexuality, class, race and spatial (dis)locations, issues with
which the different chapters are engaged; an intervention in the

nexus of social relations of production and consumption. Having outlined my own position, it is important to point out that in constructing the book I have deliberately *not* sought consensus, I have not imposed a methodology or single approach. The other writers have been free to address the questions raised by a post-modern approach in any way they saw fit. I, therefore, no more than the other contributors, necessarily agree with all the arguments and findings expressed. However, the issues raised are, I believe, significant and require engagement.

Those very few works on postmodernism that have touched on music tend to concentrate on what is generally termed 'pop' music and steer clear of the complex issues surrounding what we can refer to as 'art' music. It is this issue which Robin Hartwell takes up in his chapter. Beginning with Brahms and concluding with Schnittke, he traces a line of 'development' within the paradigms of modernism and postmodernism. Race and its relationship to contemporary sensibilities are issues addressed through different rubrics by Peter Jowers and Amon Saba Saakana. Jowers analyses the world music phenomenon within the culture of postmodernity, especially as it relates to internationalism, while Saakana takes a contentious position arguing around issues of cultural and musical appropriation. The complex surrounding music, sexuality and gender is addressed in the chapters by Alexander Laski and Derek Scott. The applicability of postmodern methodologies as they might be used in relation to gay disco music is engaged with by Laski. Scott's concern is the representation of sexuality in three different musical styles: Baroque opera, Victorian drawing-room ballads and popular music in the USA in the 1920s and 1930s. Paul Théberge's essay contextualises the role of technology: a central, practical and theoretical referent in any discussion of contemporary musical production and consumption.

Given the problems surrounding the notion of postmodernism, I believe a collection of divergent essays to be the most appropriate form for a book dealing with this subject. The book does not aim at providing answers to all the issues it raises, rather it is our aim to put a number of important questions on the agenda. The future, as always, is up for grabs. It is in my view important for musicology to enter the fight, to stake its claim and not rest content to lament the passing of traditional approaches. Of all the humanities, music could find itself best placed to trumpet the last post.

Note

1   A. L. Rees and Frances Borzello, ed., *The New Art History* (London, 1986), Introduction, p. 2. There have been a small number of books which offer alternative approaches to methodology within the study of music. Principal among them could be listed: J. Kerman, *Musicology* (London, 1985); J. Shepherd, *Music as Social Text* (London, 1991); C. Ballantine, *Music and its Social Meanings* (New York, 1984); C. Small, *Music–Society–Education* (London, 1980); A. Durant, *Conditions of Music* (London, 1984); R. Leppert and S. McClary, *Music and Society* (Cambridge and New York, 1987), R. Leppert, *Music and Image* (Cambridge, 1989); C. Norris, ed., *Music and the Politics of Culture* (London, 1989), and most recently Edward W. Said, *Musical Elaborations* (London, 1991).

Simon Miller

Towards a hermeneutics of music

The introduction of a new kind of music must be shunned as imperilling the whole state; since styles of music are never disturbed without affecting the most important political institutions.

The new style gradually gaining a lodgement, quietly insinuates itself into manners and customs; and from these it issues in greater force, and makes its way into mutual compacts; and from compacts it goes on to attack laws and constitutions, displaying the utmost impudence, until it ends by overturning everything, both in public and in private.[1]

Discussions about the nature and existence of the concept of post-modernism have been taking place for some time now. While much ink has been spilt in the analysis of the concept in general and its application to a wide field of other cultural phenomena in particular, these discussions have notably failed to engage with the relationship between postmodernism and the art of music. This is no accident, for two different but related reasons. On the one hand, most cultural commentators, while they feel equipped to discuss a range of art practices, feel ill-prepared to venture into the sound world of music. Music more obviously constitutes itself through sometimes complex 'abstract' temporal structures, which can manifest themselves through the language of notation; a system which is known but rarely directly dealt with by cultural commentators. The myth that this therefore makes it less capable of socio-cultural analysis derives in large part from the avoidance of the teaching of the basic vocabulary of music within cultural studies. The ephemeral nature of music, its temporal quality, can be overcome by learning to explain musical experience through an understanding of this language. This is most obvious with notation, but there are other means aided by the more recent developments in recording technology – for example the patient use of the cassette player. There are no insurmountable difficulties: musical sound is real and therefore open to analysis in a similar way to visual information – it is a different kind of object, but an object nevertheless.

On the other hand, most musicologists feel equally unequipped to tread a path through the complex minefield of post-structuralist theory. This problem is compounded by the formalist myopia of much musical study which concentrates too exclusively on questions of musical language, while making little attempt to see these formal concerns as connected in any way to larger socio-cultural forces.

The link between these two difficulties is the philosophical tradition upon which much music scholarship is founded. It makes discussion of meaning in music problematical, for this idealist tradition posits music above or beyond the workings of the socio-cultural processes in which modern cultural criticism is based, and disconnects questions of meaning from the world of most formal music criticism (at least as commonly practised within academia). This is to simplify two complex fields of study but in its broad sweep it is I believe accurate. A bridge-head is already under construction by some musicologists. It is the task of this book to further the crossing of this divide.

I shall argue that it is within an analysis of postmodernism that the study of music can be re-positioned to take account of the impact of 'extra-musical' forces and therefore re-engage with the social formation: to argue for a postmodernist as opposed to a modernist musicology.[2]

Within the relatively short confines of a chapter of this sort it is not possible to do more than sketch a cursory picture of the philosophical tradition mentioned above. It is my intention therefore to provide a brief survey which will attempt no more than to follow a particular line of development, and in no way pretends to cover all (or most) of the theorists in this area. Rather, I hope to provide an introduction to a set of important questions.

Platonic philosophy regarded the archetypes or the Ideas as unchanging, eternal and 'above' the universe. Below were initial blends of spirit and material, and it is here that music (and mathematics) were situated. Below these were further levels of reproduction, the site of the other arts.[3] This hierarchical distinction hinged on the initial separation of spirit from body, and was centrally important for the development of Western philosophy. It is this split which is in part responsible for the perception of music as an autonomous sphere. However, as Plato discussed at length in *The Republic*, music was seen as having a very important moral and educational role.[4] Both Plato and Aristotle were inclined to associate the various modes with different types of feeling and character: music could move the spirit. But it could do this precisely because it was more directly associated with the archetypes.

This view was taken up by the most important musical theorist of the middle ages, Boethius, in his *De Institutione Musica*.[5] He likewise invested music with considerable fundamental powers. Boethius introduced influential categories, organised in hierarchies, such as 'musica mundana' (the music of the spheres), 'musica humana' (the music of the elements, seasons and the human body) and instrumental music. This last category was to remain at the bottom of the hierarchy for a considerable time; it was not to take its place at the pinnacle until after the philosophy of Kant, as we shall see. But for Boethius the significant point was that music in its theoretical (Idealist) guise, following Plato, continued to stand in a closer relation to the laws of nature and the universe than any of the other arts.

However, an important shift occurs in the Renaissance. The actual practice of music (as opposed to its Idealist theoretical dimension) moves nearer to these supposed natural principles: music-making comes to be regarded as the living demonstration of the Ideal. The terms on which this shift took place continued to be Neoplatonic in character, but expanded to include a much broader conception of nature (owing to developments in the understanding of the natural world). Although music as an educational force and paradigm of the harmony of nature continued to hold sway, an important change came with the incorporation of dissonance and discord into the concept of harmony, alongside the traditional emphasis on beauty.

The concepts of consonance and dissonance have their roots in the theories attributed to Pythagoras (Chinese philosophy was aware simultaneously, if not before Pythagoras, of the laws associated with vibrating bodies). He is believed to have originated the view that the ratios between small numbers characterise concords – for example $1:2$, octave, $3:2$, fifth, and $4:3$, fourth. This conception was also manifest in the visual arts, especially in the ideas of Alberti, particularly in relation to architecture;[6] in this way, in the words of Wittkower, 'A familiarity with musical theory became a *sine qua non* of artistic education' for Renaissance artists and thinkers.[7] In short, and this is a point to which I shall return, music and mathematics were intimately linked: geometry was the key to the universe, and music was the geometry of sound: number made aural (perhaps most clearly seen in the work of Alberti's older contemporary Ugolino of Orvieto).[8] It was with developments in harmonic and polyphonic techniques that this tension between theory and practice became most obvious, for it was here that traditional theoretical conceptions of consonance rubbed up against the *secunda prattica* of dissonance; as a consequence a broader concept of 'natural' harmony developed. Discord became an accepted stylistic device.

Nevertheless, although Renaissance philosophy could subsume, to some extent, the polarities of consonance and dissonance, this did not mean a break with the objective science of numbers. Beauty became the result of harmony between contrasts. Perhaps the clearest practical outcome of these developments can be seen in the revision of the practice of tempering. Here less strict mathematical (though mathematical nevertheless) accordance – based more on judgements of the ear – allowed excursions from the modal norm into the area of harmonic chromaticism. This marked a shift to the systematic evaluation of experience, and brings us to the emphasis on empiricism which marked the rise of science at the birth of the modern age (or the Classical age if we follow Foucault's chronology).[9]

Whatever the nomenclature, this period is in philosophical terms most often associated with the work of Descartes. His specific writings on music continued mathematical speculation on the concepts of consonance and dissonance but in a way significantly different from earlier speculation. His earliest work *Musica compendium* (*Musical Compendium*, written in 1618, but published only after his death in 1650)[10] and his last work *Les Passions de l'âme* (*The Passions of the Soul*, published in 1649) contain his most significant contributions to music theory.[11] The *Compendium* is a mathematical study of the laws of acoustics and harmony, which does not attempt to apply them to responses, whereas the *Passions* considers the physics and physiology of affects, but without direct application to music. The important difference between Descartes' approach and earlier speculation is in his reluctance to equate mathematically derived harmony with musical pleasure. Following the shift I mentioned earlier the experience of the listener plays a more significant role: 'to determine what is most pleasant we have to know the listener's disposition, which varies, like taste, from person to person'.[12]

Significantly he differentiated between the simplicity, the harmony of a consonance, and its 'agreeableness'. This had the effect of placing the affects of music firmly within the soul (within fixed categories), and it is because of the dualism of the soul (mind) and the body (world), as he famously postulated them, that a distance is maintained from the world (the everyday), and therefore the epistemological division I have so far described – between music and social life – continued to hold sway.

The music theorist Johann Mattheson should also be briefly mentioned, for he is perhaps the most significant musical empiricist of the eighteenth century.[13] He modelled his ideas on the writings of Locke and Bacon, and delivered a considerable blow to Pythagorean notions of the primacy of mathematics in music, pursuing and greatly extending the role of experience that I mentioned above in reference to Descartes. The basis of his argument was that since everything in the mind must first enter through the senses – science originating in observation – the ear is the prime judge of all musical experiences: 'the sense of hearing resident in the soul [is] the best judge in this matter'.[14] Therefore, he argued, previous reliance on mathematics for music was, in short, misguided. Although this may appear to contradict my assertions so far – for it is contrary to the numerological emphasis of the Pythagorian tradition – it is I believe consistent in at least one important respect. It is the other side of the same epistemological coin, for in its positioning of the unmediated soul at the heart of the understanding of musical experiences it maintains separation. Mattheson is left relying heavily on the Cartesian concept of passions, which, as I have already mentioned, limits understanding to questions of taste and the 'natural' sensibilities of each individual. Nevertheless, the mathematically informed approach to music was soon to reassert itself. Its most well known and influential rebirth was brought about by the early Enlightenment composer and theorist Jean-Phillippe Rameau.

As mentioned above, the importance of mathematically derived theories of music lies in their perceived natural, objective and universal validity. Rameau is particularly important in the emphasis he placed on the primacy of reason over experience. This distinguishes him from empiricists like Mattheson and links him to the mathematically inspired Cartesian tradition. His ideas, as expressed primarily in his less than lucid *Traité de l'harmonie* (*Treatise on Harmony*, 1722 which has the significant additional phrase, *Reduced to its natural principles*), show him to be an archetypal Enlightenment thinker through his reliance on science as a validating system, where reason is validated by experience:

The surviving writings of the Ancients show us clearly that reason alone enabled them to discover most of the properties of music. Although experience still obliges us to accept the greater part of their rules, we neglect today all the advantages to be derived from the use of reason in favour of purely practical experience . . .

Music is a science which should have definite rules; these rules should be drawn from an evident principle; and this principle cannot really be known without the aid of mathematics. Notwithstanding all the experience I may have acquired in music from being associated with it for so long, I must confess that only with the aid of mathematics did my ideas become clear and did light replace a certain obscurity of which I was unaware before.[15]

By reference to the wisdom of the ancients, Rameau draws a line of historical progress. He validates his position by rooting it in the past, adding his derivation of rules based on the natural principles of vibrating bodies (*corps sonore*). The mathematical precision and rational justification of his ideas together contribute to split, in Cartesian terms, the body (experience) from the mind (reason/ intellect), and in musical terms place the triad as the foundation of harmony. Such an approach helps to present his argument as both historically justifiable, 'natural', and therefore by implication, morally good. These notions are all in general central to the Enlightenment project, and therefore important to understanding the attack postmodernism has launched against this conception. I shall return to this challenge, but first I will continue the brief historical survey of the theoretical arguments which have acted to hold music aloof from the workings of everyday life and experience.

Kant's complex philosophy emerged out of the rationalism of Descartes and the empiricism of Locke and Hume. No attempt here will be made to summarise Kant's ideas (any more than those of the other philosophers so far discussed); rather we shall be concerned only with the core of his arguments as they affect the present discussion – music and its relationship to social life. As already discussed, instrumental music (music in its most 'abstract' form) was most often regarded as inferior to other forms of music. This was because questions of content (and therefore control over meaning) were seen as most problematic in relation to determining the true nature of this branch of the art. In other words, exact readings of meaning were not possible except in relation to language (libretto); instrumental music had no fixed signified and therefore could affect the passions but in the process bypassed conscious understanding. This is not to argue that music was up to this time considered to be autonomous in relation to the world and nature, rather that it had a particular relationship which maintained a type of separation. For example, within the Pythagorian tradition music was seen as having, through number, a natural relation with nature and the universe, but one at such a level of abstraction that it stood in an ideal, rather than real (everyday), relationship to human life, as a mimesis of the archetypes. Kant is important to our argument because he freed (instrumental) music, and allowed it to be 'honestly' autonomous. He distinguishes between two forms of beauty in his *Critique of Judgement* – free beauty and dependent beauty:

The first presupposes no concept of what the object ought to be; the second does presuppose such a concept and the perfection of the object therein . . . foliage for borders or wall papers, mean nothing in themselves; they represent nothing – no object under a definite concept – and are free beauties. We can refer to the same class what are called in music phantasies (i.e. pieces without any theme), and in fact all music without words.

In the judging of a free beauty (according to the mere form), the judgement of taste is pure.[16]

This formalist emancipation for music from language also frees music from concepts. As a result it ranks at the bottom of artistic hierarchies for Kant, because of this perceived conceptual poverty. This is important because as a result music becomes paradigmatic in another way: it is both subjective and universal. Music (and art) has become separated from the cognitive and moral spheres of influence, it affects our feelings but not our minds:

[the art of tone] . . . speaks by means of mere sensation without concepts, and so does not, like poetry, leave anything over for reflection . . . It is, however, rather enjoyment than cultivation (the further play of thought that is excited by its means is merely the effect of a, as it were, mechanical association), and in the judgement of reason it has less worth than any other of the beautiful arts.[17]

Kant's argument, though not his pejorative placing of music within an artistic hierarchy, was to have a profound effect on future generations of theorists. Within Romanticism music's autonomous nature was to justify its place as paradigmatic among the arts: as Schiller expressed it: 'The plastic arts, at their most perfect, must become music and move us by the immediacy of their sensuous presence.'[18] Writers such as Tieck, Wackenroder, and E. T. A. Hoffmann argued that symphonic instrumental music ('absolute music' as Wagner coined the term) was the art of arts because of its perceived innocence of reference to the external world, and its power to suggest because of its indefinite nature.

The emphasis placed on the subjective power of music within Idealist philosophy of necessity regards music as objectless and immediate in its effects. However, as I mentioned at the outset of this chapter music is an object; it exists outside, external to the subject – although this is not to argue that meaning is inherent in the object, except in a limited formal sense (as physical character-istics); it is rather constituted through contexts of production and reception. As Lucy Green has recently argued:

The subject structures its intentions towards music according to what it knows of music. If confounded by processual change in the musical structure, subjective intentionality is negated and restructured on the basis of new knowledge; if realised by the musical structure, intentionality is processually affirmed.[19]

In other words music is a temporal structure, one that is com-prehended on the basis of previous knowledge (particularly in terms of an understanding of categories of style). Listening to music is an exploratory process that involves both memory and the anticipation of future events. The conceptual error, of not con-ceiving of music as an object, not only allows music to be conceived as autonomous from the world (of objects), but as we have seen, also leaves it conceptless, or to put it more strongly, meaningless.

This bypassing of reason and cognitive processes is clearly seen in Schopenhauer's writings on music. For him music is paradigmatic precisely because of this condition; music intuitively presents the will or is indeed the will made audible. We have thus arrived back, albeit by a different route, at a Neoplatonic conception of music as directly (or closely) connected with the archetypes: in Schopenhauer's words, whereas the other arts 'speak only of shadows', music 'speaks of the thing itself'.[20] It is not only the will speaking, it is speaking a truer language. Therefore music is not only independent of spoken/written language, it is an art beyond words and representation, it is paradoxically a model for poetry because it has broken free of the chains of rational everyday discourse. Romantic discussion of the arts resounds with such statements, but perhaps the best known characterisation of this tendency is to be found in the writings of Walter Pater.

Art, then, is thus always striving to be independent of the mere intelligence, to become a matter of pure perception . . . It is the art of music which most completely realises this artistic ideal, this perfect identification of matter and form . . . and one of the chief functions of aesthetic criticism dealing with the products of art, new or old, is to estimate the degree in which each of those products approaches, in this sense, to musical law.[21]

This split, between rationality, meaning etc., and a notion of 'pure' unmediated expression or perception, places the emphasis on individual (individualistic) responses; music has certain affects *in* us. Music is therefore more 'natural' when nature is taken to mean, in the words of A. O. Lovejoy, those inborn attributes 'which are most spontaneous, unpremeditated, untouched by reflection or design, and free from the bondage of social convention'.[22] Music is, in other words, true metaphysics. The important point about such a universalising subjectivity is that the subject is most often conceived of as having no sex/gender, race, age, prior beliefs or knowledge, rather it is just a collection of organs capable of unmediated response; universal, asocial beings. So although emphasis has been placed on individual response, this is a response which fits smoothly alongside, or rather forms a constituent element of, bourgeois (individualist) ideology where the particular is unique. A materialist musicology must challenge this, it must consider rather the ways in which music opens up the experience of others, how it makes connections, and contributes to the construction of common sen-

sibilities. This last point is important in the consideration of
another significant aspect of Romanticism to which I shall now
briefly turn (before I return to the question of a materialist
musicology), that is the role of music in the rise of nationalisms in
the later part of the nineteenth century.

The eighteenth century had seen the consolidation, in Europe, of
powerful oppressive autocracies. The development of free market
ideologies towards the end of the eighteenth and beginning of the
nineteenth centuries saw the extension of inequalities into a system
where those who controlled the means of production controlled the
means of social definition (symbolic production). Music played an
important part in the establishment of race and national consciousness in opposition to such dominant views, and through such
concepts as *Volksgeist* placed the potential for the development of
alternative senses of identity in, among other things, 'folk' music.[23]
As well as the political motivation for this interest, an important
factor driving this concern with 'folk' material originates in the
Romantic desire to get nearer to the 'primitive' roots of things; in
the words of Percy Scholes it was 'at one and the same time a "my
country" motive and a "back to the land" motive'.[24] It is easy
to overemphasise the emotive character of Romanticism at the
expense of formal elements (the art for art's sake conception – the
pure play of form), for a metaphysical Pythagorean aesthetic is an
important aspect of some Romantic musical theory (for example in
Novalis's *Allgemeines Brouillon.*[25]) Nevertheless, the emphasis on
individual expression gave rise to a theodicy which moved artists
and their art to the centre, and this in its turn placed a concern
with the ethical within the aesthetic (the two united by the concept
of taste), but a personal (genius), as opposed to a social, ethic. A
morality reached by aesthetic insight, rather than rational reasoning
(an anathema to Kant): the artist acting and expressing on behalf
of his or her audience, the work recreating the original feeling
through empathy. Music was thus seen as the consummate art in
the way it connected form and expression (see Pater above). This
ethic was, following the Enlightenment, informed by an approach
to nature which equated the natural with the good. It followed that
the search for identity in the multifarious varieties of vernacular
('folk') music, and the emphasis on emotional expression, led to the
introduction into (Western) art music of new rhythmic, melodic
and harmonic phraseologies. This created musical languages which

were hybrid and culturally specific, and against which modernists reacted by seeking a more classically 'pure' and 'universal' form of expression.[26]

The central figure in modernist debates about the nature and role of music is Theodor W. Adorno. He expanded the sociological/ musicological initiatives of Max Weber, who in his *The Rational and Social Foundations of Music* (published in 1921, but written around 1911)[27] marks an important point in the development of the study of music by challenging the Idealist conception we have so far considered. Before turning to a brief consideration of Adorno's writings, it is worth summarising the arguments of Weber's music criticism, as they are not generally well known. He was concerned to demonstrate that social, economic and technical features all contributed to the development of Western music, leading to its rationalisation into systems of harmony (tonality), twelve equal tempered notes, and specific instrumentation. This rationalisation process stems, according to Weber, from the concomitant evolution of music into a profession. It is the rationalisation of harmony into a complex system of tonality (the rules governing the disposition of chords) that is its most distinctive feature, and which has played such an important role in structuring Western hearing. For, he argues, it is only through such a central placement of tonal laws that the development of atonality could take place in the early years of the present century. It is through the development of notation that such control could be exerted over such large forces (the symphony orchestra); increasingly music was planned ever more closely. The notation system with which we are familiar (five-line stave) has led to considerable control over time-pitch parameters, but significantly less control over other areas of sound, notably timbre. It has often been the case that other musics, which place emphasis on the elements over which our system gives least control, have been viewed, as a consequence, as inferior. This rationalisation process has therefore, according to Weber, created a tension between the Western tradition and 'irrational', 'primitive' (defined from a Western perspective) music.

Schoenberg in his book *Theory of Harmony* (published in 1911, around the same year as Weber was writing his work)[28] pursued a related line of argument. He proposed that notions of consonance and dissonance were relative: 'dissonances are nothing else but more remote consonances'.[29] In other words, he suggested that

Western harmonic music was not a closed natural system, but one which was dynamic and open to change and development. And it was of course Schoenberg who was the 'hero' of Adorno's musicological arguments, to which I shall now turn.

In his book *Philosophy of Modern Music* (written over the years 1939–48)[30] Adorno argued that music was a historical rather than a simply mathematical, natural phenomenon. As such it is intimately connected with wider social issues, which it unselfconsciously 're-presents'. Adorno's book explores the 'crisis' of modern(ist) music, and considers Schoenberg as its arbiter and paradigm. The nature of this crisis is dependent on the notion of a collapse in the validity of tonality as the unifying force of Western art music; Schoenberg is regarded as the one who fulfilled the necessities of the historical situation – the move from tonality into atonality. He took, Adorno argues, Romantic subjectivity to an extreme, through his development of musical form and language. He therefore, according to Adorno, breaks through expressionism to a form of aesthetic objectivity. The self is abandoned, but it is abandoned in anguish. It is his music, in other words, which makes apparent the 'ugliness' of modern alienated life (the 'negative dialectic'). However, with the later development of the twelve-note system Schoenberg's music becomes for Adorno emblematic of, or reproduces in its internal logic, an increasingly rationalised and repressive social world: the apogee of rationalisation, as described by Weber.

In order for music to reclaim a sense of aesthetic objectivity, after the developments in musical language mapped out above in relation to Romanticism, a differentiation of spheres was necessary – the uncoupling of art from political and economic systems: *Ausdifferenzierung* as Habermas has characterised it.[31] This is precisely what happened as a consequence of the early stages of capitalist modernisation. However, it should also be noted that this strategy of exclusion was challenged as soon as it arose. The irony, as Huyssen among others has pointed out, is that this break from church and state which allows for separate spheres of high autonomous art on the one hand, and mass culture on the other, was only possible when art was first organised according to the principles of market economy; as Eagleton has put it:

When art becomes a commodity, it is released from its traditional social functions within church, court and state into the autonomous freedom of the market place. Now it exists, not for any specific audience, but just for anybody with the taste to appreciate it and the money to buy it. And in so far as it exists for nothing and nobody in particular, it can be said to exist for itself. It is 'independent' because it has been swallowed up by commodity production.[32]

I would add, in passing, that this situation was exacerbated by the emergence of utilitarianism as the guiding philosophy of the bourgeoisie in early industrial Britain. For utilitarianism, in a crude or popular form, placed the arts on the periphery of society where they were able to engage in aesthetic questions concerning the human spirit and other such individual/instinctual conditions but, because the arts were perceived as non-utilitarian in nature, they were unable to engage legitimately in cognitive, ethical and political concerns, as these issues were better dealt with in other spheres of social life (e.g. science, philosophy and government). This is to add a historical dimension to the argument Adorno and Horkheimer first postulated in relation to what they called 'the culture industry' in their book *Dialectic of Enlightenment*.[33] This aestheticism has particular resonance in relation to music, which, I have argued, had maintained a form of separation through Idealist thinking. This needs to be seen in the context of the shifts that took place within modernism and the avant-garde, for as Adorno points out, 'Contrary to past styles, it [modernism] does not negate earlier art forms; it negates tradition per se'.[34] It is therefore the avant-garde (as opposed to modernism) which seeks to reintegrate art and life, and in music this can perhaps be seen most clearly in the work and ideas of a number of early avant-garde Soviet composers; principal among them Nikolai Andreevich Roslavets (1881–1944).[35] Here dodecaphonic solutions to problems of musical organisation were allied to Marxist–Leninist forms of cultural expression; new non-hierarchical artistic practices for a non-hierarchical social system (at least in theory). However, as Huyssen has argued, the notion of a politically committed art is an anathema for Adorno whose work, he further suggests,

holds in charged tension two diverging tendencies: on the one hand aestheticism's insistence on the autonomy of the art work and its double-layered separateness from everyday life (separate as work of art and separate in its refusal of realistic representation) and, on the other, the avantgarde's radical break with precisely that tradition of art's autonomy. In doing so he delivers the work's autonomy to the social while preserving it at the same time: 'Art's double character, its being autonomous and *fait social*, relentlessly pervades the zone of its autonomy.' Simultaneously he radicalizes modernity's break with the past and with tradition in the spirit of avantgardism.[36]

It is important to appreciate the reasons Adorno (and Clement Greenberg, who was writing on modernism at the same time) had for maintaining this separation. It springs from the political impulse to rescue the dignity and autonomy of art works from the manipulation of art/culture in the hands of fascism, Stalinism and the capitalist culture industry: the same hands that effectively strangled the political/radical life out of the avant-garde.

Before we turn our attention to more contemporary musical concerns it is worth briefly surveying the ideas of a musician who worked closely with Adorno, one who was passionately involved in the development of a socially committed 'serious' form of musical expression: Hanns Eisler.

Eisler wrote: 'The reluctance of the musician to think outside his art is an exact description of the special feature of the music'.[37] His attempts to rectify this fault as he saw it, to transmit music and politics together, led to the development of *angewandte Musik*, for his advice to young composers was: 'For a time really try to do without inflated symphonic music, playful chamber music and esoteric poetry. Choose texts and subjects that concern as many people as possible'.[38] This use of texts was for Eisler a way of making the content/meaning of his music more explicit (an issue we considered above); he did not believe that the acquisition of modern musical techniques of composition, and the understanding of the development of Western art music which he had studied under his teacher Schoenberg, were sufficient for composing music that had the serious social function he thought worthy of it. Therefore the explicit links music could/should make with other aspects of life could only be directly achieved through the primacy of the text; it is here that he worked closely with Brecht.

Central to Eisler's aesthetic was the notion that the transformation of musical material should not be carried out without full cognisance of the function of the music, nor of the (modernist) conception of the evolution of the genre, nor importantly, the processes of listening. Reception was therefore contingent on the development of society. Dissonance for Eisler must therefore be perceived with an awareness of its social ramifications; its effect relying on processes of listening. Eisler relates the homogenising role of tonal music (as conceived by Adorno) to the reception characteristics of musical listening environments, especially that of the concert hall. It is the passive reception of music which Eisler feels should be transformed, as he writes in his essay 'The Crisis in Music' of 1935:

The opinion is frequently heard that music by its very nature is not able to effect changes in the social life of man. However, it must be pointed out that this opinion has only arisen out of a peculiar practice over the last hundred years and previously was seldom voiced.

The history of Chinese music, of European music in the Middle Ages and of our own time shows that music has attempted again and again, more or less consciously, to play a part in social life.

If the composer today claims that music has no social or political function, he merely reveals his ignorance of these functions . . . In fact music not only serves certain social functions, but allows of a change in these functions, so that it is then made to serve an aim different than that for which it was written . . . Instead of trying to bring about a state of psychic stupefaction or chaotic excitement in the listener, music must endeavour to clarify the consciousness of the most advanced class, the working class, and must attempt to influence the practical actions of the audience.[39]

Such a programme is unlike Adorno in that focus is placed more clearly on the processes of production and consumption, rather than on formal procedures. Important questions are raised about participation, training and organisation: who is to play what, where, and under what conditions. Eisler continues the project of relativity, arguing that musical effects (and meanings) are dependent not only on the formal/stylistic context of production but also on the social contexts, specifically the institutions, of production and reception. The central point here is that music is seen as an object which can mediate, rather than just reflect, social relationships. Contextual meaning therefore becomes fluid and negotiation of meaning becomes possible. This is fundamental, I would suggest, to the development of a critical materialist musicology. It is this question to which I shall now turn in a consideration of more contemporary issues.

Classical modernism emerged as a strategy of exclusion, but such a position of aesthetic autonomy was challenged by the historical

avant-garde (or anti-modernists) who attempted to develop alternative strategies by looking to alternative cultural traditions, as
we have seen in the works of Eisler. However, the failure of this
move has left us with the same type of divisions discussed above.
The division within musicology between 'high' and 'low' culture,
between art and discourses of politics or ethics: both of these are as
clear in the academies today as they were in the nineteenth century.
If musicology is to escape such a modernist process of exclusion, its
belief in innate 'quality' and its concern with contamination must
be challenged through theories of postmodernism, which hold part
of the solution to a more inclusive, less paranoid form of cultural
appraisal: one which regards questions of worth as bound up in the
areas of social life which have been so trenchantly held apart from
the effects of music.

In his book *Postmodern Culture*[40] Hal Foster argues for what he
calls a postmodernism of resistance, a position which is predicated
on a recognition, or celebration, of diversity and difference. It is
within such an understanding of 'otherness' that a new musicology
should be situated. In this way an intervention in the emergence of
subjectivity, gender, class and race, and spatial (dis)locations can
be made, which disrupts the *telos* of Idealism. A materialist study
of music recognises the relationship between meaning, power and
authority. I am not suggesting that postmodernism is some form of
universal remedy for all the ills of modernist discourse; nor for that
matter that modernism is all bad, a cancer that must be wholly
removed from the body of musicology in order to restore health.
For I conclude that postmodernism is in many ways a crisis in the
broad history of modernism, rather than a complete break from
it. It is a form of discourse that emphasises the fragmentary,
the ephemeral. It looks with scepticism at prescriptions of eternal
and immutable forms of legitimation (what Lyotard refers to as
'metanarratives'). It demonstrates the difficulties of communication, and related to this the complexity and subtle shades of
interests, sensibilities, cultural context that are the experience of
individuals, the 'multiple forms of otherness', to quote Huyssen.[41]
All of this can have a positive effect on the methodologies of
cultural studies, but there are dangers.

The clearest epistemological difficulty is described by David
Harvey:

Obsessed with deconstruction and delegitimating every form of argument they [postmodernist philosophers] encounter, they can end only in condemning their own validity claims to a point where nothing remains of any basis for reasoned action . . . Worst of all, while it opens up a radical prospect by acknowledging the authenticity of other voices, postmodernist thinking immediately shuts off those voices from access to more universal sources of power by ghettoizing them with opaque otherness . . . It therefore disempowers those voices . . . in a world of lop-sided power relations.[42]

The problem is largely one of methodology. It is important to be cognisant of the problems set up within postmodernist discourses, but that need not necessarily mean that a contemporary materialist musicology should accept all aspects of poststructuralist philosophy. Indeed I would argue that while notions of meaning can be seen as in flux, it is nevertheless important to maintain a political cutting edge by tying down meanings within the framework of shifting power relations. In other words, starting from a recognition of difference and 'otherness', musicology should play a part in the recuperation of social categories such as race, gender and class. For it is with the use of such 'open' (not fixed and universal) categories that power can be challenged – in terms of an open-ended and dialectical mode of enquiry. Music is a part of the symbolic order, not something above or beyond it. A materialist musicology, which recognises the positive contribution of postmodernism, can progress to show how music plays a part in the construction of sensibilities, social distinctions, etc.; music is a fundamental part of the nexus formed by history/culture/society.

This is all rather general so I shall attempt to provide a more specific account by looking in more detail at contemporary music and theory.

In a more recent discussion between Michel Foucault and Pierre Boulez, 'Contemporary Music and the Public',[43] the question of the relationship between music and other areas of culture is addressed. It is argued that the inaccessibility of avant-garde music is caused largely by our nostalgia for the past. Points similar to those made above are discussed: the links between music and technological changes, the role of what Foucault calls 'rock' music and lifestyle – 'Not only is rock music (much more than jazz used to be) an integral part of the life of many people, but it is a cultural initiator: to like rock, to like a certain kind of rock rather than another, is also a way of life, a manner of reacting; it is a whole set of tastes and attitudes.' He goes on:

One cannot speak of a single relation of contemporary culture to music in general, but of a tolerance, more or less benevolent, with regard to a plurality of musics. Each is granted the 'right' to existence, and the right is perceived as an equality of worth. Each is worth as much as the group which practices it or recognizes it. [44]

In response Boulez argues that such a 'liberal' attitude erases values and consolidates ghettoes. This returns us to the position of the role of critical intervention. I would suggest that in order for musicology to account for, say, the qualitative difference between Andrew Lloyd Webber and Stephen Sondheim, Michael Tippett and John Adams, John Zorn and James Brown, Pink Floyd and The Farm, Bob Marley and Samuel Coleridge-Taylor, or Mozart and any of the above, it needs to address directly the contexts of production and consumption. Questions of meaning(s) in music are culturally relative. Creativity and emotional responses are shaped by the world in which the creators (recipients) lived, by her/his desires, personal attitudes and relationships, by complex psychological factors and equally complex socio-cultural forces. But these complexities should not be allowed to paralyse us. For creativity is also constrained or encouraged by the tastes of society, tastes which are also shaped by psychological and socio-cultural forces; by technological facilities and by the accessibility/comprehensibility of musical styles and languages. The latter are already well investigated by musicology, although focus is often directed only at certain types of music. Part of the 'postmodern condition' is felt in the world of expanded communications. The contact we can now have with a range of different musics brings home the diversity of meaning and challenges the notion of universal subjectivity and what counts as music for different individuals.

This is not an argument for a sociology of music, for one already exists. Rather, I am suggesting that a 'new' musicology would be fruitful, one which did not acknowledge a distinction between formal analysis (empirical) and contextual analysis (sociological); history, politics, socio-cultural circumstances should not be viewed as autotomous from detailed textual phenomena. Likewise it is questionable whether so called ethnomusicology should be regarded as a discipline separate from other forms of music study. One person's peripheral culture is another's mainstream.

It has not only been popular musics (Afro-American) which have in more recent times been influenced by musics outside the Western mainstream. The music of Philip Glass, for example, has learnt from Javanese gamelan (in a way technically and contextually very different from Debussy earlier in the century) and Indian classical musics. In his turn Glass has composed for 'pop' musicians (*Songs from Liquid Days*), opera (*Einstein on the Beach*), the overtly eclectic Kronos Quartet, and others. Closer to home Michael Nyman uses Mozart, Purcell and rock music as well as manipulations of his own previous output to feed into his compositions. In the 'pop' field, not only have we recently been inundated by a plethora of nostalgic re-releases and cover-versions, but the 'group' Enigma, for example recently had a number one single which featured plainsong ('Sadness, Part One'). The questions of parody and pastiche – common in postmodern parlance[45] – are made even more complex in the case of music by variation technique, transcription and more recently by sampling (facilitated by new technologies). Anyone who believes that 'musical quotation' began with Schnittke or Grand Master Flash has not listened to Mahler, or the Masses of Palestrina. I am not suggesting that musical quotes and paraphrases mean the same thing in different musical contexts; precisely the opposite: one needs to be aware of the complexities involved and not fall into the trap of overgeneralising disparate cultural and historical phenomena. The central issue is how to conceptualise critical listening in the face of such an explosion of musical languages; how to avoid the 'anything goes', everything-can-be-plundered cultural 'tourism' of a decontextualised musical practice. I do not wish to appear prescriptive. It is important to remain open to trial, error and debate. Nevertheless I feel it is imperative to abandon the dead-end dichotomy of music versus politics, autonomy versus society, along with any other mutually exclusive categories.

If modernist musicology uses such oppositions – tradition/ innovation, 'high'/'low' culture, reaction/progress, right/left, etc. – then a postmodern musicology does not deny them. Rather, it operates across such boundaries in a way which does not automatically privilege one over the other (à *la* Derrida). It should not mean the complete reversal of the modernist project, to a point where the former of the two terms is contrarily privileged over the latter. The tension created by such 'oppositions' is exactly the dynamic which is needed to revitalise musicology. If anything, it should be heightened.

Notes

1 Plato, *The Republic* Book 4, 424. I am grateful to Milto Frangopoulos for clarifying the translation of certain key concepts.
2 I use the term 'musicology' to stand for the study of music in a broad sense, as opposed to its more restricted use to define formal analysis (as against music history/sociology). I shall argue that such divisions are unhelpful, and therefore require rethinking; a new methodology is needed.
3 See Plato, *Timaeus*.
4 See *The Republic*, esp. Part 2, Books 2–4, 398–403.
5 See Umberto Eco, *Art and Beauty in the Middle Ages*, translated by Hugh Bredin (New Haven, Conn., 1986), esp. Chapter III.
6 Alberti's main source was Vitruvius, who also inspired Boethius, for whom mathematics was no less a central organising principle. See also Wittkower, *Architectural Principles in the Age of Humanism* (London, 4th edition, 1973). For a clear explanation of the harmonic/overtone series see Bernstein *The Unanswered Question: Six Talks at Harvard* (Cambridge, Mass., 1976), esp. pp. 17–25.
7 Wittkower, p. 117.
8 Ugolino of Orvieto (*c.* 1380 – after 1457), composer and theoretician. See Albert Seay 'Ugolino of Orvieto Theorist and Composer', *Musica Disciplina*, vol. IX. I have also found Dorothy Koeningsberger's *Renaissance Man and Creative Thinking: A History of Concepts of Harmony 1400–1700* (Brighton, 1979) useful to my discussion.
9 Michel Foucault *The Order of Things* (London, 1970).
10 René Descartes *Musicae compendium*, 1650 (Darmstadt, 1978).
11 Descartes, *Les passions de l'âme*, 1649 (Paris, 1970).
12 *Correspondence*, vol. III, quoted after John Neubauer's *The Emancipation of Music from Language: Departure from Mimesis in Eighteenth-Century Aesthetics* (New Havens 1986, p. 48). This work also proved useful to parts of my discussion.
13 For a more detailed discussion see Neubauer.
14 Quoted after Neubauer, p. 19.
15 *Treatise on Harmony*, translated with introduction and notes by Philip Gossett (New York, 1971) pp. xxxiii and xxxv.
16 Immanuel Kant *Critique of Judgement*, translated by J. H. Bernard (London 1914), first book, section 16, part 1.
17 Kant, second book, section 53, part 1. As the focus of my argument is on questions of social significance, rather than directly with questions of aesthetics, I have had to leave aside a number of important

thinkers. But in relation to Kant it is worth mentioning that Hegel too regarded music as 'patterns of sound', an art that was cognitivly non-expanding. (see Jack Kaminsky, *Hegel on Art* (New York, 1962), pp. 118–30 and Lucy Green, *Music on Deaf Ears: Musical Meaning, Ideology and Education* (Manchester, 1988), pp. 12–16).

18 Friedrich Schiller, *On the Aesthetic Education of Man*, edited and translated by Elizabeth M. Wilkinson and L. A. Willoughby (Oxford, 1967, reprint 1982), p. 155, twenty-second letter.

19 Green, p. 16.

20 Schopenhauer, *The World as Will and Representation*, 1819 (2 vols, New York, 1969), Book II, paragraph 52.

21 Walter Pater, *The Renaissance* (Oxford, reprint 1986), pp. 88–9.

22 A. O. Lovejoy, 'On the Discrimination of Romanticisms', in *Essays in the History of Ideas* (Baltimore, Md., 1948), p. 238.

23 For a critique of the concept of 'folk' music see Dave Harker, *Fakesong* (Milton Keynes, 1985).

24 Percy Scholes, *The Oxford Companion to Music*, 10th edition (London, 1970), p. 673.

25 Novalis wrote in *Allgemeines Brouillon*:

> Musical mathematics.
>   Doesn't music contain some combinational analysis and vice versa?
>   Numerical-harmonics, number-acoustics belong to combinational analysis.
>   [. . .] Combinational analysis leads to number-fantasies and teaches the compositional art of numbers, the mathematical cyphered base. (Pythagoras. Leibnitz) Language is a musical idea instrument. The poet, the rhetorician, and the philosopher play and compose grammatically. (III, 360)

See John Neubauer, *Novalis* (Boston, Mass., 1980): 'Novalis' main contribution was to recognise that the analogy between music and the new poetry rested on the non-referential nature of their signs. Precisely this feature brought music and poetry into the proximity of algebra' (p. 54).

26 Derek B. Scott has recently argued that the use of 'peasant music' by Bartók offered the composer a way out of the 'major–minor' crisis. It provided a modernist sense of progress offering 'new' chordal and melodic materials. See *The Musical Quarterly*, vol. 74, no. 3 (1990), p. 395.

27 Max Weber, *The Rational and Social Foundations of Music*, translated by D. Martindale et al. (Carbondale, NY, 1969).

28 Arnold Schoenberg, *Theory of Harmony*, translated by Roy E. Carter (London, 1978).

29 Schoenberg, p. 21 (Chapter III).

30 Theodor Adorno, *Philosophy of Modern Music*, translated by A. Mitchell and W. Bloomster (New York, 1973).

31 See Jürgen Habermas, *Strukturwandel der Öffentlichkeit* (Berlin, 1962).

32 Terry Eagleton, *The Ideology of the Aesthetic* (Oxford, 1990), p. 368.

33 Adorno, *Dialectic of Enlightenment*, with Horkheimer, translated by John Cumming (London, 1973).

34   Adorno, *Asthetische Theorie* (Frankfurt am Main, 1970), p. 16.
35   See Simon Miller, 'Music and Art and the Crisis in Early Modernism'
     (Unpublished Ph.D., University of Essex, 1988).
36   Andreas Huyssen, *After the Great Divide* (London and New York,
     1986), p. 32.
37   Quoted after Albrecht Betz, *Hanns Eisler: Political Musician*
     (Cambridge, 1982), p. 242.
38   Hanns Eisler, *A Rebel in Music: Selected Writings*, edited by M. Grabs
     (Berlin, 1978), p. 30.
39   Ibid., pp. 115–16.
40   Hal Foster, ed., *Postmodern Culture* (London, 1985).
41   See Huyssen, p. 219.
42   David Harvey, *The Condition of Postmodernity* (Oxford, 1989), pp.
     116–17. This book provides an excellent discussion which can serve
     as, but is more than, an introduction to the paradigms modern (ity/
     ism) and postmodern (ity/ism).
43   *Michel Foucault, Politics, Philosophy, Culture: Interviews and Other
     Writing 1977–1984*, edited and introduced by Lawrence D. Kritzman
     (London, 1988).
44   Ibid., p. 316.
45   Fredric Jameson, 'Postmodernism, or the Cultural Logic of
     Capitalism', *New Left Review*, no. 146 (July/August 1984), esp. pp.
     64–5.

Robin Hartwell

Postmodernism and art music

The 1980s have seen the increase of the use of the term *postmodernism* in the criticism of the arts. The exact meaning of the term has lacked a single definition, and is still capable of different meanings. This looseness of prescribed meaning has enabled commentators to apply the term to numerous different musical styles, some less radical than others, and across a wide portion of twentieth-century music. The term advertises the death of modernism, an event oddly difficult to pin-point.

Andreas Huyssen, writing in 1981, says that;

> the term 'postmodernism' will variously refer to American art movements from pop to performance, to recent experimentalism in dance, theatre and fiction, and to certain avant-gardist trends in literary criticism from the work of Leslie Fiedler and Susan Sontag in the 1960's to the more recent appropriation of French cultural theory by American critics who may or may not call themselves postmodernists.[1]

The source of one difficulty (and one which Huyssen addresses eloquently) is to describe 'modernism', and to distinguish it from its brother, the avant-garde. As he points out, for many the terms blur into one another, to the extent that 'Renato Poggioli's *Theory of the Avant-garde* . . . was reviewed in the United States as if it were a book about modernism, and John Weightman's *The Concept of the Avant-garde* of 1973 is subtitled *Explorations in Modernism*'.

For the purposes of indicating the cultural shift I observe to have taken place in the last decade, and which, Humpty-Dumpty style, I wish to call postmodernism, I shall emphasise the close relationship between modernism and the avant-garde, based on the way that both the idea of an avant-garde, in theoretical terms, and a fundamental assumption of modernism, rely on a shared awareness of history. Specifically, I wish to assert that the term *avant-garde* is reliant on the idea that there is a direction to history, and the avant-garde is that brave group of pioneers leading the way from the present into the future.

In the morass of writing on modernism there is a huge variety of definitions and categorisations of the term *modernism*. Given this, I shall unpick certain strands within modernism as a movement, with the understanding that the resultant picture may conflict with well-regarded and authoritative views of the movement. This picture will, of necessity, be partial. I shall insist that postmodernism is best seen as part of the modernist line, and not as a capitulation of modernism to a version of Classicism.

One task, then, is to describe those aspects of modernism which postmodernism seeks to revoke, and to describe the means by which this is to be achieved. Another is to describe how the phenomenon of modernism came to be applied to one branch of music, for this itself forms part of a historical process.

Self-consciousness concerning history

I see modernism as the conjunction of two forces. One of these is the result of an ever-increasing rise in historical consciousness, indeed in historical self-consciousness. This can be associated with the rise of the notion of the *Zeitgeist*; that there is a mode of expression appropriate to, and rooted in, a specific historical and social situation. It might be expected that such an idea, based on a notion of communality, would result in a single, common, artistic language, but the rise of the notion of the *Zeitgeist* occurs at the same time as an increasingly subjective and idiosyncratic use, if not, indeed, actual creation, of musical language. Broadly, I am referring to a shift from the eighteenth century, where the grammar of harmony was common to most composers and originality lay in its usage, through Wagner, where the musical grammar itself was valued for its originality, to the twentieth century, where the basic materials of music – chords, tone-colours etc. – are perceived as the intellectual property of particular composers. (For example, one has the sensation that Messiaen has patented certain modes, chord formations and orchestral colours. To work with these materials is to run the danger of committing an act of plagiarism.)

If I am correct in understanding this as a shift in the perception of how the individuality and worth of a composer are to be judged, it might be thought that this provides a model for the fragmentation of commonly used means of communication, thus working in direct opposition to the idea of the *Zeitgeist*. This is not so. For this very subjectivity is not opposed to the expression of the historical moment, but, being itself formed by it, is rather the truest expression of that moment. The expressionist phase of art can be seen as the attempt to create an individual, unmediated language; to capture the present, freed from the distortions of received knowledge; to find in the descent from the conscious into the subconscious a flight from the pressure of the past into the unmediated present. Yet expressionism is now a perceptibly aesthetic position located within a continuum of artistic history.

At the basis of modernism is the assumption that there should be a relationship between art and the age in which it is produced. Consequently, the art of the twentieth century will be necessarily different from the art of previous epochs. One can see that this notion requires a self-conscious understanding of one's position within a historical continuum, which here is characterised as a chain of irreversible changes. Thus, those who have the most acute sense of being in the present will have, paradoxically, the strongest sense of the past. For modernism and the avant-garde the past demonstrates change and tranformation, rather than truths or transcendent values which are fixed through the ages. While awareness of the past is necessary for the formation of historical consciousness, the response of the avant-garde is to attempt a break with the past, to institute a new order. This is in contrast to classical values, which see in history the demonstration of constancies, specifically of aesthetic judgement, deriving from the universality of human nature.

It is on this issue, based on the wider social attitude to the idea of progress, and, more amorphously, on the teleological nature of history, that I wish to focus for a moment. The belief in progress, central to Enlightenment thinking, Habermas has characterised as 'the belief, inspired by modern science, in the infinite progress of knowledge, and in the infinite advance towards social and moral betterment'.[2]

The phenomenon of the collapse in the belief in the avant-garde typifies the general crisis of the role of history in the present, particularly the notion of progress, which has been central to artistic and political thought. (I hesitantly point out the collapse of Marxist states in Eastern Europe, the rise of Green politics with limited economic growth, conservation, the rise of a museum culture . . . never was the past so popular.)

It is the change of attitude to the past which has marked out a significant segment of the music of the last few decades and it is this shift to which I wish to give the name postmodernism.

Self-consciousness concerning language

Within modernism one can trace the ever-strengthening power of the rational. This appears to have little in common with the irrational basis of expressionist and surrealist art, both part of modernism. However, we should be wary of this apparent opposition, for the history of the second Viennese school – from expressionism to serialism, pointing towards, in the case of Webern, an extreme of constructivism – appears to be the beginning of a new project on a new aesthetic base. Serialism marks a revolutionary break. Indeed, it would be quite wrong to minimise this, especially given Schoenberg's commitment to the notion of the *Zeitgeist*. But if it is correct to place both phases of the second Viennese school, the expressionist and the serial, within modernism, one would expect them to hold some things in common. I would identify this as an acute self-consciousness concerning language.

This manifests itself in an idea featured in both atonality and serialism: that it is within the power of the composer to create his own musical language. And this notwithstanding Schoenbergs attempts to present himself as the vessel through which historical necessity poured itself. The contradiction in Schoenberg's wanting to have his musical language recognised as a universal language while remaining his own individual language is a dilemma at the heart of the avant-garde position, and is illustrated by Schoenberg's response to Thomas Mann's description of the twelve-tone system in his novel *Dr Faustus*. Mann had taken advice on the technique of composition with twelve tones from Adorno, and attributed the invention of this method to his fictional hero, Adrian Leverkühn, in the novel *Doctor Faustus*. Schoenberg was distressed to hear of this appropriation, writing to Josef Rufer that 'he [Mann] had attributed my 12-note method to his hero, without mentioning my name. I drew his attention to the fact that historians might make use of this to do me an injustice. After prolonged reluctance he declared himself prepared to insert, in all subsequent copies in all languages, a statement concerning my being the originator of this method.' This incident shows Schoenberg's belief that his musical language was his personal discovery or creation, and his depth of feeling on the matter is shown by his refusal to allow his intellectual property to be used even by a fictional character.[3]

The new self-consciousness concerning how and what language communicates is another mark of modernism, and significantly runs alongside the development of the discipline of linguistics. A theoretical expression of the autonomy of language is found in Saussure's *General Course on Linguistics*, where natural language is seen as an enclosed system of signs. The implication for the creative artist is that, given the arbitrary relation between the signifier and the signified, and that language is grammatically and semantically contained within the boundaries of the system of signs, then the creation of an idiosyncratic system of signs becomes a possibility. The communicativeness of such a work, if indeed it were to be of any concern of the artist, would be guaranteed by the innate ability of the human mind to construct an abstract grammar from particular concrete instances.

The second strand, then, which I wish to locate within modernism is the belief that grammar can be invented by an artist, and is not something necessarily dependent on either a unmediated connection between the sign and the world or a system of conventional signs passed down historically within society.

The melancholy or nihilistic strand

I would wish to associate this nihilism with the formation of historical consciousness; to see the desire to obliterate the past as a reaction to the presence of history. The most extreme manifestations of this tendency in avant-garde art are less clear in music than in many other art forms. Poggioli outlines this nihilistic stance as 'the point of extreme tension reached by antagonism toward the public and tradition; doubtless its true significance is a revolt of the modern artist against the spiritual and social ambience in which he is destined to be born and to grow and to die'.[4]

As a specific instance of this tendency Poggioli cites Dadaism, and within music the work of John Cage comes closest to these ideals, especially given the influence of Satie on Cage. Without moving to this extreme one can remember Schoenberg's longing for a large audience, together with his disdain for the masses. The loneliness which the avant-garde position engenders is tangled up with antagonism towards society as a two-way process. Similarly the ideal of an easy understanding between composer and audience is at odds with the perceived necessity for a new language.

Distinguishing postmodernism from Neoclassicism

It may be useful at this stage to see how the characteristics which I have selected as typifying modernism can be distinguished from the Classicist attitude. The reader will excuse, I hope, a long quotation from Poggioli:

To a superficial observer, the romantic idea of the *Zeitgeist* in fact appears almost as a modern variation of the myth of the fullness of time. But that myth is static, whereas the *Zeitgeist* myth is dynamic. The fundamental principle of the latter is that every age attains the fullness of its own time, not by being, but by becoming, not in terms of its own self but of its relative historical mission and hence of history as an absolute. This means for the moderns the consciousness of historical culmination, or the fullness of time, is at once granted or denied to each epoch, pertaining to none or to all. In the consciousness of a classical epoch, it is not the present that brings the past to a culmination, but the past that culminates in the present, and the present is in its turn understood as a new triumph of ancient and eternal values, as a return to the principles of the true and the just, as a restoration or rebirth of those principles.[5]

The issue concerns the relation of the present to the past, and it has been exactly this which has marked a cultural shift away from modernism, under the name postmodernism. The problem is to understand whether the position of postmodernism is a variant of Neoclassicism (as is suggested by the title *Postmodernism: the New Classicism in Art and Architecture* by Charles Jencks, London, 1987), and what its distinguishing characteristics would be.

From modernism to postmodernism

One can characterise the shift from modernism to postmodernism as a shift from a position of antagonism towards the past to one of appropriation. This antagonism, in avant-garde art, is seen as overt rejection, but in the broader stream of modernism the attitude to the past provides the crucial test. 'Modern' music is music which is separated off from music of the past, creating two broad categories of music: modern music and non-modern music. One can see these two categories as mutually dependent, and it has been pointed out that the rise of modernism and of authentic performance practice of music of the past occurred simultaneously. Significantly, they share many characteristics. The distinction between modernists and authentic music revivalists is that one values the music of the present as a manifestation of the present, and the other wishes to establish music of the past in the present. But both emphasise the historical position of the artwork. What I wish to call post-modernism seeks to show this construction of historical perspective as an artifice, and insists on the 'presentness' of any experience.

This aesthetic shift reassesses the value and positions of historical products in the present. It is a shift from a modernist position, which relegates the products of the past to the past (or at least places the past as found in the present under the category of 'history'), to the understanding of all cultural products as equally extant in the present, and all styles as equally possibly and valid.

As a guiding principle I shall understand by modernism that (1) art is capable of historical transformation; that (2) these transformations are necessary, and either reflect progress or embody social truths and relationships (in either case new art is demanded by a new age); and that (3) modernism sees the past as leading to the present, and judges the past by the standards of the present. One can crudely distinguish this from classicism, which judges the present by standards abstracted from the past. The values found in modernism may, however, be similarly historically transcendent, and in this sense classic (one thinks of expressionism). Modernism is reliant on a view of history which values change in history rather than continuity. These changes may (or not) have positive values, called progress, or necessity, or truth. This force, seen either as progress or simply as the dictates of the *Zeitgeist*, takes on the status of a moral imperative. Postmodernism abolishes this moral dimension.

The need for modernists to revalue the music of the past is clear. The quantity of music performed from the past, made available by technology and the market, together with the existence of or expanding class of cultural consumers, has led to the position where contemporary art music is one product amongst many, and a product without any distinguishing social or economic function. One could say that the 1980s were the time when quantity of choice together with the establishment of a taste for historical music led to the position of new art music was no longer felt to command any authority. Further, the process of historical revival was so established as a cultural phenomenon that the demand for novelty could be satisfied by musicological research rather than by the composition of new pieces. The realisation that the history of art does not need to be teleological robbed art music of the assumption that an audience for the avant-garde would inevitably follow in the course of time. The realisation came that there was no compulsion for the contemporary audience to concern itself with contemporary music. Nor need it do so in the future. The avant-garde had battled ahead, but no one was inclined to follow.

The rise (and fall?) of authentic performance

One must wonder at the seeming coincidence of the availability of the whole history of Western art music and the arrival of postmodernism. Indeed, the connection between the revival of early music, particularly in the twentieth-century phase when this was concerned with the revival of earlier performance practices, and the rise of modernism itself, has been noted. Richard Taruskin, in 'The Pastness of the Present', expresses the opinion that 'the ideal of authentic performance grew up alongside modernism, shares its tenets, and will probably decline alongside it as well. Its values, its justification, and, yes, its authenticity, will only be revealed in conjunction with those of modernism'.[6]

Indeed it is a constant theme in the chapters in this book that the notion of historically accurate (and so in this sense authentic) performance is generally attacked by those very people at the centre of the authentic performance movement. If this leads to a post-authentic performance practice movement, which is the logical conclusion of many of the arguments put forward here, then the historical eras of modernism and authenticity will be precisely chronologically coincident. And so surely not coincidental.

While the expression of postmodernism can be seen in the music of various composers and performers, others remain totally identified with the modernist creed. It is not simply that modernism is dead and postmodernism stands in its stead.

This can be observed in Boulez's attitude to the music of the past in the repertoire he chooses to perform as a conductor. On the one hand one notes that it is concerned largely with those works of the modernist mainstream, especially the second Viennese school, but even within this there are certain preferences. Boulez is thoroughgoing enough to have qualms about those works of Schoenberg which show the influence of a Neoclassic aesthetic, and one feels that works such as the Piano Concerto are valued by Boulez for their use of serial language, rather than their concern for establishing links with the European past, in particular the music of Brahms. Thus Boulez repeatedly returns to works of the expressionist period. A similar attitude can be seen in Boulez's forays into music of the nineteenth century, where it is clear he is happier with the music of Wagner, as a progressive, than with Brahms, seen as a conservative. Where Brahms is admitted into the canon it is in the Serenades, works in which he was attempting to stand outside the force of tradition as represented by the symphony.

The basis of Boulez's aesthetic position has been characterised by Habermas: 'whatever can survive time has always been considered to be a classic. But the emphatically modern document no longer borrows this power of being a classic from the authority of a past epoch; instead, a modern work becomes a classic because it had once been authentically modern'.[7]

Thus works are to be valued according to how progressive they were at the time of their production. In this they provide both examples of previous modernisms and a lineage of avant-garde saints justifying the position of the present-day avant-garde.

Boulez's compositions are consistent with the view of history discernible in his performances. That is, there is an elaboration of a musical language based on the purification of the style he developed after the Second World War, recently combined with the use of the most sophisticated technology that modern society can provide. Concerns with the internal integrity of language, combined with the use of the instruments of the age, are quintessentially modernistic.

Thus while Boulez may be observed to be holding to the modernist line, the revision of the modernist position under pressure from the quantity of music by past composers appears as postmodernism. The term itself is a paradox: the position appears to adopt an ahistorical stance, but is itself the latest thing, and the term refers both to the passage of time as seen in change (*post*) and to a historically defined concept (*modernism*). And it is modernism which seems most wedded to the idea of progress, of transformation in time, which postmodernism now progresses beyond.

The rise of musical historiography and a museum culture

The process of historical accumulation is not, of course, a phenomenon of the 1980s. One can trace the growth in the availability of non-contemporary music at least as far back as the beginning of the nineteenth century. The present historical consciousness itself has a history.

A useful tool in tracing the rise of historical thinking within music is Warren Dwight Allen's *Philosophies of Music History*.[8] His avowed aim is the 'pursuit not of men but of assumptions, in the tracking down of persistent notions'.[9] The book is in two parts. The first is a historical survey, from 'The First Three Histories in German, Italian and French' to music history since 1900. The second attempts to extract the key concepts which underlie the writing of music history.

I wish to draw two observations from the book. The first is the explosion in the quantity of writing on the history of music. While the 'three first books to bear the general description History of Music' appear within the period 1690–1715, Allen estimates that 'between 1850 and 1900, there appeared as many histories in Germany alone as had appeared in all the years previous in all countries'.[10]

The first interest in the history of music can be associated with the rise of Enlightenment thought and, significantly, the rise of the notion of progress, which Allen dates from about 1690.[11] It is the gradual penetration of this idea into historiography which marks its transformation through the nineteenth century. That is, the model of history moves from a description of fixed periods in music history through to one which sees music as changing organically through time.

One strand is the notion of progress. Allen traces this from Herbert Spencer's article 'The Origins of Music' of 1854, which is presented as one of his Illustrations of Universal Progress. (One notes that Darwin's *The Origin of Species* was not published till

1859, some four years later. The point is that the notion of progress is itself a part of the *Zeitgeist*.) Allen summarises different approaches to the idea of progress: 'The notion of progress upwards has been illustrated in the theories of Fischer and Lavignac, who saw the history of music in terms of spiral ascent; in Schopenhauer's mystic scale of Will-Development from the bass upward; in Wagner's assertion that harmony grows upward like a pillar, and in the theories of upward growth of harmony and folk music from roots'.[12]

Thus within musical culture two forces are in play: one is the rise in the importance of musicology, the other is that a guiding, if not moral, principle can be derived from it. Whether the lesson to be drawn is that the art of music is in a state of perpetual progress, heading towards a glorious future, or that it is in a state of organic decline from a glorious past, is a matter of differing opinions. What unites them is a consciousness of the present situated within a historical continuum, and that this consciousness would be impossible without the historicisation of the culture.

This is to give an account of the educational and intellectual side of musical culture. Yet the same expansion of the past into the present can be observed in music practice, and can be seen to operate in two ways. Firstly, the music of the Classical period has been maintained in the performing repertoire from the time of its production to the present day. Unlike the music which preceded it, which was discarded by society as outmoded within a short space of time, this music was retained to form the core of a standard repertoire. As the nineteenth century progressed the corpus of work permitted to enter the museum of the concert hall accumulated. But there was a second source of music for this imaginary museum, namely the recovery of neglected works of previous centuries. Thus one can imagine the repertoire expanding both backwards and forwards in time from the late Classical period. As this expansion occurred, cultural energy, meaning musicology and performance, was expended less on contemporary music, and the musical culture became one where the music of the past was the central concern, with newly written music becoming the preserve of the eccentric. It is an astonishing reversal, giving rise to a change in our understanding of what is the true subject of musical culture, in a way unimaginable in any other art-form.

This situation is compounded in the twentieth century by the growth of a technology which makes available music in performance to a mass audience. Increasingly, musical culture rests less on the social role of music, where individual choice may even be a disrupting factor, and more on diversity of choice, maximised through technology and market forces, which enhances individual freedom to choose. Thus it is possible to be perfectly active in one of the sub-sets of musical life in society without having any connection with contemporary compositions. In fact, for that segment of society interested in art music, this is the commonest position.[13]

One should also underline the peculiarity of music as an art-form in this regard. An equivalent might be a sub-set of contemporary theatres which play only revivals. In the fine arts the situation is somewhat different, for while there appears to be a similar divide between the study of the historical aspect of the subject and those involved in contemporary production of art, a moment's reflection will show that were architects to behave like concert pianists, with the majority reproducing the styles of the eighteenth and nineteenth centuries, then the incorporation of elements drawn from earlier historical styles would have much less impact, not to mention meeting with less antagonism. In art music the situation is much less clear-cut than in other art forms, especially those forms where traces of postmodernism are easily identifiable.

The response of Brahms to the rise in historical consciousness in the nineteenth century

Thus the expansion of the past in the present had already been faced in the nineteenth century. The choices were three: (1) to believe in the progressive nature of new art and its role in the future; (2) to believe that music had, at the moment of this crisis, reached its perfected form and to admit of no further technical change; (3) to incorporate the past within contemporary composition.

I see (1) as leading to the notion of the avant-garde, from Liszt to Boulez. The stance is typified by the desire to expunge (as inauthentic) the past from the present; (2) results in the values of academicism; (3) is the least explored position, but runs as a thread through the nineteenth century, playing a significant role in the formation of Brahms's musical language in particular. It is also the position of postmodernism.

Brahms's music has, even from the time of its production, been recognised as belonging to the Classical line, in opposition to the progressive music of the New German School of Wagner and Liszt. Brahms's music has been seen as traditional, in the sense that it maintains elements of earlier music, transforming the language of Beethoven and Schumann only slightly. The relationship to the music of the immediate past is not one of identical style, which would correspond to a static notion of Classicism, but permits some development while maintaining the same form.

The image of Brahms is shifting, thanks in no small part to the work of Virginia Hancock. In her book on Brahms's choral music and his library of early music,[14] she traces the close connection between Brahms's interest in specific pieces of 'early music' and his own compositions. This relationship is most noticeable in the choral music, where the medium is the same as much of the revived music. However, it is clear that Brahms was not concerned just with the music of the immediate past, Schumann, Schubert and Beethoven, but also made close contact with music of the more distant past. By the time of his death his library contained the complete editions of the works of J. S. Bach (1685–1750), Handel (1685–1759) and Schütz (1585–1672), and music by Lotti (1667–1740), Corelli (1653–1713), G. Gabrieli (1557–1612), Clemens non Papa (c. 1510 – c. 1556/8), Lassus (1532–94) and Palestrina (1525–94). Thus he had built up a detailed knowledge of music stretching back through the eighteenth and seventeenth centuries into the sixteenth.

Hancock is at pains to point out that Brahms absorbs elements of the compositional style of these pieces into his own musical language.[15] She writes 'This song ["Ich schell mein Horn"], along with another composed at about the same time, "Vergangen ist mir Glück und Heil", . . . are the only examples in Brahms's published choral output where he appears to have deliberately attempted imitations of sixteenth century polyphonic Lieder', so downplaying the most extreme examples of Brahms's imitation in this genre. But one can express this the other way round, and say that there are two occasions where Brahms is prepared to write in a deliberately anachronistic style, to authorise these as his own, and even to produce them in two versions: they also appear in versions for voice and piano, as part of the two song collections of op. 43/3 and op. 48/6.

These works stand as a challenge to the idea of *Zeitgeist*. Hancock

seems to be suggesting that the works are acceptable to the extent
that they deviate from their historical models, but describes these
differences, conversely, in terms of the transformation of this historical style into Brahms's own.[16] For the sake of clarification I
shall identify those characteristics. Of prime importance is Brahms's
involvement with counterpoint and modality. Hancock points out
that his first choral compositions (about 1854) are canons, the most
strictly contrapuntal form conceivable. She identifies a possible
source for one of these, 'the Palestrina of Clara Schumann's A 134
copies', and notes that it does not fully conform to the musical
grammar of Palestrina's time, 'The anachronistic dominant seventh
in the fourth-to-last bar'.[17]

With a growing awareness of the music of the sixteenth century,
Brahms would have become conscious of the possibility of diluting
the forces inherent in the tonal system with the weaker gravita-
tional forces of modality. Brahms met the older modes in both the
revival of ancient music and the folk melodies he harmonised.
Hancock identifies a relationship to Praetorius in the *Marienlieder*
op. 22, and points out the melody in the Dorian mode in 'Marias
Kirchgesang'. Again, Hancock feels it necessary to distance Brahms
from his influences: 'That Brahms was not attempting to write a
mere imitation of sixteenth century style is shown clearly by his
setting of no. 4, "Der Jäger," an attractive and purely Romantic
hunting song full of secondary dominants.'

With the three choral songs op. 42 Hancock refers us to the issue
I am attempting to elucidate: 'in these three pieces, with their
varying influences, we see most clearly Brahms's "central artistic
problem," the reconciliation of the divergent principles of historic-
ism and nineteenth century Romanticism.'[18]

She quotes Hans Gal as saying that 'Vineta' (op. 42/2) begins and
ends like an antiphonal chorus of the sixteenth century but has a
middle section in the romantic lieder style. And yet, because the
musical construction flows so naturally from the words and their
expression, one never has any sensation of discrepancy'.[19]

Writing on the motets op. 29 Hancock says:

if we are to speak of a principal early music 'influence' on these motets it
must be Bach's cantatas 4 and 21, which Brahms had performed with the
Detmold choir in 1858 and 1859 . . . In 'Es ist das Heil' (op. 29/1), Brahms
follows a fairly straightforward chorale setting in the style of Bach by a
chorale motet with cantus firmus in which nearly every available contra-

puntal device is used. . . . In particular, Brahms's chorale motet resembles Bach's verse 4 [of Cantata 4], 'Es war ein Wunderlicher Krieg,' in an astonishing number of details.[20]

By the time of the middle period of Brahms's music, 1865–85, Hancock finds it harder to locate the precise sources of Brahms's inspiration. She writes, 'By the time the work was complete [the German Requiem, completed in 1867] he has so thoroughly incorporated techniques learned from this study into his own style that countless examples may be found throughout it, and indeed in all his compositions'.[21] Specifically she points out the use of recitative, text-painting, rhythmic ambiguities (including hemiolas), and canonic techniques, 'which are clearly derived from Baroque practice'.[22]

A return to a style in which a direct relationship to early music can be seen in Brahms's late period (1886–9), of which Hancock says: 'It may indeed be the case that Brahms's sudden activity in writing works for a cappella mixed chorus with large numbers was stimulated by the Schütz edition, especially by the polychoral Psalmen Davids'.[23] The complete Schütz edition, to which Brahms was a subscriber, began to appear in 1885.

Thus the picture we can extract of Brahms's music is one in which the music of the past can be detected, sometimes with precision, sometimes as a tendency. It is a paradox of the nineteenth century that the rise of historical consciousness is part of the spirit of the age, so the moment when Brahms is most anachronistic is the moment when he most accurately captures one aspect of the *Zeitgeist*.

In this respect Brahms can be seen as prefiguring, as a pre-modernist, one aspect of postmodernism. For there is no distinct category of pieces which can be separated off as pastiche works, or works which recast the music of the past in the materials of the present, but rather there is a continuum of compositional usage of musical techniques from the past. These range from the most obvious to pieces which have the surface of late-Romantic art works but have hidden in their compositional underpinning techniques of writing derived from the music of the past. In the fact that they utilise these techniques, which would be available only with the revival of early music, they are absolutely 'modern' and of their time.

The dilemma, which we also meet in postmodern music, is whether this use of music from the past falls within a Classicist aesthetic, appealing to eternal verities and a naturalistic view of musical grammar, or should be more radically understood as a contemporary device, which the contemporary composer is perfectly free to utilise, either in its entirety or as a modification of traditional musical language.

We can draw from this some points to give the context of the present transformation of modernism into postmodernism.

The seeds of modernism grew up at the same time as the historicisation of musical culture. The response of Liszt and Wagner can be seen as the desire to hold to a notion of a strictly linear view of the history of music, whereby the notion of progress could be maintained through a line of tradition, which rarely sought inspiration from a past more distant than the previous generation. Brahms, on the other hand, sought not only to conserve the forms of the previous generation (in fact a generation slightly more removed than this, for the forms of instrumental music were a full hundred years old by the time of Brahms's maturity) but to leap across the historical divide and subvert the strict chronology of history by incorporating compositional styles which had been discarded by the linear process of tradition. Inevitably this led – sometimes even within a single work – towards 'polystylism'. In Brahms's case this conflict led in the direction of synthesis, a new coherence and in effect a kind of Neoclassicism. Nevertheless, a full understanding of his musical language is impossible without taking into account the revival of earlier music. With the advent of postmodernism it is tempting to interpret Brahms' music from the point of view of discontinuities, ignoring any smoothness of the surface. The present crisis of the historicisation of musical culture has its own history, and at the moment of its birth Brahms foresaw the consequences. Only now can we see that, in turning to the music of the past, Brahms most accurately captured the spirit of his present.

The use of the music of the past in the music of the present

Though the postmodern piece of music utilises musical language from the past, it is not with the intention of resurrecting this mode as a living language but rather to represent to the listener the artificiality of the language, demonstrating the distance between the signifier and the signified. To distinguish itself from Neoclassicism, which would insist on a natural relation between the signifier and the signified, the surface of the postmodern work must distort and fragment language, juxtaposing variant forms of language against each other, to prevent the focus moving from the surface of the sign to the signified.

While the Neoclassical artist makes references to the past to endorse values in the present, the postmodernist quotes the past in order to underline the distance between the sign and its meaning. For the Classicist, language is coherent, guaranteed by the unchanging human subject. For the postmodernist, language is seen as that which constitutes the the subject. Thus within post-modernism it is impossible to judge the falsity of a musical language as it is language which bestows authenticity. Truth, obliquely and provisionally, must be expressed by a juxtaposition of contradictory discourses, as an exposition of the constituent elements of sub-jectivity. The project changes from that of a search for an authentic language (meaning one that expresses the *Zeitgeist*), in contrast to a corrupted language, to a demonstration of the incompatibility of musical languages, without the projection of any one of these as being of higher value. Thus the subject is not centred in one position, from which a degree of relative authenticity can be meas-ured, but exists in a network of possibilities in which the value system changes with the change in perspective.

In one sense this prolongs the death throes of modernism, for as well as relying on a tradition which is concerned with the problem of language and meaning, it also maintains 'the experience of mobility in society, acceleration in history, of discontinuity in everyday life', which Habermas has seen as characterising modern-ism.[24] It is an intensification of the modern condition, for while 'The new value placed on the transitory, the elusive, and the ephemeral, the very celebration of dynamism, discloses the longing for an undefiled, an immaculate and stable present',[25] the post-modern art work reminds us of that desire, only to withhold the consolation which we would gain from the internal coherence of a work from the past. Indeed, such music, by placing within itself the many musical languages in which we enjoy competence, reveals to us the constructive role we play in decoding these works. That no one single code is sufficient – including the primary code that the art work should be a unity – marks an attack on the past as a privileged category. While the incorporation of multiple codes within the art work distinguishes the postmodern from the modern, it can still be related to the same tradition, for it was an attribute of modernism that it had, at its extremes, 'the anarchistic intention of blowing up the continuum of history', that it 'lives on the experience of rebelling against all that is normative', and 'is addicted to the fascination of that horror which accompanies the act of profaning'.[26]

At its crudest, works identified as postmodern hold in common the utilisation of a number of musical styles within the same piece, or of a musical language that refers to premodern music.

The number and variety of the composers who can be related to postmodernism depends on how far back, historically, the commentator wishes to identify the use of quotation as a postmodernist phenomenon. In effect, the sudden interest in quotation and pastiche has resulted in the construction of a new historical line, which can be read back from Schnittke, through B. A. Zimmermann and Peter Maxwell Davies to Stravinsky and other Neoclassical composers, perhaps even to Charles Ives. It could also include Berg's Violin Concerto, Bartók's Sixth String Quartet and Schoenberg's Second String Quartet.

This interpretation of the term is a cause for worry, as it creates a postmodernist line running alongside modernism, and not following it in historical succession. Appealing though it is to have one's system of categories presented in the same ahistorical manner as its subject, it hardly seems worth the resultant confusion, given that all that is then meant is non-modernism, or perhaps anti-modernism. Further, the distinction between Schoenberg and Stravinsky, which seems so central to our understanding of the first half of the twentieth century, is made even more blurred than before.

To be able to identify a work as postmodern, I would suggest that we must be able to separate those works which utilise styles of the past as exemplars of Classical meaning from those which present the surface of the style without wishing to authorise the meaning they carry. While that meaning can still be read, it has to be understood as something constructed, its original certainty now buried under layers of irony. Thus I would see postmodernism as dealing in negations of the meaning of music. It is not that all musical languages are available as means of expression, but rather that all musical languages exemplify the distance between the signifier and the signified.

One can now tentatively outline the continuity between modernism and postmodernism. Postmodernism is a response to the increasing historicisation of Western culture, combined with a scrutiny of the means by which language conveys meaning. Under this pressure the integrity of a single musical language is no longer tenable, so that the plurality of contemporary musical languages are juxtaposed within the same frame. However, in distinction to Brahms (the premodernist), where the attempt was made to cover the discontinuities, postmodernism emphasised the consistent incompatibilities of musical discourses. Both modernism and postmodernism insist on the isolation of the individual and of self-consciousness concerning the use of language. In modernism this led to the creation of an ever more individualised language. In postmodernism even the guarantee of meaning by interior subjectivity evaporates, so that all that remains is a play of empty signs, the flotsam of the past bobbing on the ocean of the present. This position is fraught with multiple irony, and one can never be absolutely sure which side of the coin, if any, is authorised.

Is it possible to identify a musical work as being postmodern?

I can see no way forward except that of testing each case. I would set the following criteria, which presuppose that the work contains stylistic incongruities. (1) If the use of a past historical style appears to be endorsed, or is to be read as the continuation of a tradition, then the work has Classical tendencies. (2) If the work opposes an alien style to a seemingly modern style then this can read as part of the aesthetics of modernism. And finally (3), if no one style seems to be authorised, but there is a play of contrasting styles, then one may have postmodernism.

Clearly this cannot be objective, and many commentators, including Habermas, do not admit the last category, and group all works of this type as a variety of Neoconservatism.

The first category contains the music of Stravinsky. For Stravinsky the past is seen as repository of styles, but each style still carries a residue of meaning into the present. However, in its self-conscious searching through the past for the meaning in musical styles, Stravinsky's music (I refer to the works from

Pulcinella to *The Rake's Progress*) is considerably more modernistic than, say, that of Vaughan Williams or William Walton, which seems to propose a direct relation between language and meaning without incorporating historical mediation within the art work itself. The difficulty is to distinguish between Stravinsky's use of past historical styles within Neoclassicism and a hypothetical post-modern music. I would make the following observations. Firstly, those works by Stravinsky which can be identified with specific historical precedents do not appear as pastiche works. They present the music as if through a distorting screen, and the presence of these distortions provides the means whereby the historical position of the composer can be identified. Secondly, the relationship of the composer to the historical material can be distinguished from that of the line of Brahms and Schoenberg. In this German line there is a strand of pessimism, of nostalgia, of a sense of loss, of separation from the past. In Stravinsky's music, even through the distorting screen, the past is still sweetly meaningful in the present, not saturated in bitter irony.

The second category of style, where the stylistic incongruities are to be judged from the standpoint of an authentic language, is visible as early as Schoenberg's Second String Quartet of 1908. This work is one of the first pieces to abandon tonality, and breaks further with tradition by adding a soprano soloist to the small chamber ensemble. In the second movement Schoenberg writes into the music the melody 'Ach, du Lieber Augustin'. This can be understood as having a autobiographical aspect, in that the words to the song end 'all is lost', which could relate to Schoenberg's domestic crisis. In stylistic terms it appears as an anomaly, from a different harmonic world from the rest of the quartet. It is clear, for reasons of proportion, that this is an intrusion, and that the easily comprehensible language of the song is to be understood ironically, as a kind of stupidity. Interestingly, Schoenberg then dissolves the melody into the atonal texture, so that the melody appears with the maximum degree of shock and is then reduced into the pervasive style of the piece. The implication is that the atonal style is the authentic voice of the composer, while the song is inauthentic.

This can be distinguished from Berg's use of the Bach chorale 'Es ist genug' in his Violin Concerto (1935). Once again we have a work which is somewhat removed from functional tonal language, into which a tonal fragment is introduced. As before, an interpretation can be made through the words that customarily go with the melody. Further, the same technique of dissolving the melody into the general style follows the chorale's introduction. However, the shock is lessened, partly owing to the way that the theme can be connected with the serial procedures in the piece, partly because the chorale is harmonically the most complex and obscure to be found in Bach, and certainly because the work maintains from the start a palpable relationship with tonality. Thus the chorale appears as the most extreme and the most tonal moment within the work. Its use is less ironic than in the Schoenberg example, in direct proportion to its similarity to the language of the concerto. The distance between the two works places the Berg that much nearer to Classicism.

The same attitude to musical language reappears after the Second World War in the music of Peter Maxwell Davies. In *Antechrist* (1967) one finds a return to something like the expressionism of Schoenberg, but at the close of the piece the appearance of the antichrist is associated with a foxtrot. It is a simple equation: the more 'modern' the musical language, the greater the authenticity.

If these examples indicate an axis allowing the incorporation of the past into a modernist art work while countering a drift towards Neoclassicism, are there any works which can be recognised as postmodernist?

The best contender for the position of post-modernist is Alfred Schnittke. His music became the most fashionable new music in the late 1980s. He has been involved in a great deal of work in film, a discipline which has enabled him to develop great fluency in many different styles. Several factors have favoured his rise: he was taken as an example of the new openness in Soviet society, his music contains much quotation and pastiche, and can be taken by less sophisticated audiences at face value. The more sophisticated may indulge in the delights of postmodernism.

What Schnittke thinks of the postmodern interpretation of his music remains unclear. There is some evidence to suggest that he is more interested in pluralism as the manifestation of greater unity, perhaps along the lines of Charles Ives, or that he believes that emotional intensity is authentic at each moment, no matter what the musical style. Further, it is becoming clear that he is only one of a number of composers in the former USSR who are using

polystylism as a compositional technique. It is possible that when
he begins to merge into a larger social and historical frame his
music will appear less revolutionary than it does in the context of
Western European modernism.

As an example of Schnittke's work I would like to consider his
Third String Quartet of 1983. The medium alone places the work
within a historical and cultural tradition. The work is cast in the
form of three movements, though not in the traditional fast – slow
– fast pattern. It juxtaposes fragments from the Stabat Mater of
Lassus with the main theme of Beethoven's Grosse Fuge, as well
as tonal and atonal chords as yet unidentified, but Mahler and
Shostakovich are possibilities. A manic waltz reappears, with an
effect reminiscent of Mahler, or the tavern scene in Berg's *Wozzeck*.
The strategy of the piece is to take the widest range of musical
styles, from the purity of the Renaissance to expressionism, and
proceed by gestures. These include: the continuance of one style
leading to the creation of a unvariegated texture; the intercutting of
two historically distinct styles; the extension of a fragment by
repetition or sequence, often with an increase in tension leading to
on abrupt switch to another musical language; the presentation of
two styles simultaneously; and passages in one style which are
unexpectedly concluded in another.

The effect is of a desperate search for an authentic stylistic voice,
each musical style being found insufficient. In the course of this the
themes are manipulated into a succession of guises, but as the
themes recur later, seemingly unaffected by these transformations,
the effect is not one of integration into a dominant language, but of
a criss-crossing of space in which these stylistic fragments appear as
landmarks.

The attraction of this music is partly due to the emotional intensity which permeates its every note. The conflict comes from the
different worlds from which the historical styles are drawn. In their
purest presentation as direct quotation, they carry with them a
reminiscence of the emotional charge of the original, which nevertheless has the appearance of being fully authorised by Schnittke.
On one level the transformation of these quotations can be read as a
criticism of contemporary consciousness, fragments of the past
appearing as a lost world of authentic emotion, viewed with a heavy
nostalgia. Alternatively, these fragments can represent the past as a
lure, reducing the search for authentic expression in the present to
gestural repetition of old motifs. Read one way it is the 'historical'

styles which act as a reproach to the 'contemporary', but read the other way the 'contemporary' style is the standpoint from which one observes the 'historical'.

Alternatively, it is possible to read all moments in the work as equally authorised. One might understand the presence of quotation as part of the interior portrayal of the composer, which includes these direct reminiscences of other composers' works. In this model, where musical works are seen as the expression of an interior world, the system of signification includes the overt representation of memories, rather than the past being subsumed within a unitary style in which history appears as tradition. Thus, these quoted fragments would carry meanings peculiar to the composer, perhaps with autobiographical significances. In effect, the quotations would operate as signs within a metalanguage, with no necessary relationship between the applied codification and the codes previously used to interpret the fragment.

Or one could attempt to understand the work as if these fragments were not quotations, but coincidentally and irrelevantly happened to sound like earlier works.

Or it is possible to attribute to the composer full consciousness of his material, in that the quotations are acknowledged as such, carrying with them a fully resonating historical context, yet remaining fully authorised by the composer. To rephrase this to connect with the pessimistic line in modernism, they are just as authorised, as sincere and as meaningful as anything else. In the case of Schnittke's Third Quartet, there is still the possibility of identifying a consistent position in the work: that of desperation, which acts as an authorial position permitting a unitary reading. Yet because this theme of desperation is expressed through a variety of incompatible styles, emphasis is thrown back on to the means by which the emotion is projected: the surface of the language, rather than the meaning itself. The means of signification is presented as part of the signifying process, and the beauty of the work is the way it is both passionate and dispassionate at the same moment.

Final comment

The use of a variety of musical styles within a single work attacks the aesthetic of the unity of the art work. This notion of unity rests on the authorisation of the work by the subjectivity of a single

artist. The postmodern work accepts the modernist position of the
arbitrary connection between the sign and the signifier, but does
not offer the consolation that we at least are coherent within ourselves, seeking the sign which we lack in order to explain ourselves
to ourselves. Neither can we force the sign to bear our meaning.
On the contrary, we are an inconsistent, incoherent mixture of
external forces, absorbed to varying degrees. Postmodernist music
is mimetic in that it attempts to present a picture of this incoherence
and the play of these forces.

Such pluralism can be associated with the return of that albatross
of modernism, the maxim of Dostoyevsky: 'If God does not exist,
then everything is permitted.' For him, at least, one senses that this
was posed as a moral dilemma. But it is this total amorality which
postmodernism now accepts. It marks another stage of the fall into
the black hole of nihilism, and much of the hostility which postmodernist art has inspired arises from an awareness of the anti-
humanitarianism to which nihilism can lead. That it stems from a
liberal position of endorsing pluralism compounds the poignancy.

Notes

1 Andreas Huyssen, 'The Search for Tradition: Avant-garde and Postmodernism in the 1970's', *New German Critique*, no. 22 (Winter
   1981), p. 23.
2 Jürgen Habermas, 'Modernity versus Postmodernity', *New German
   Critique*, no. 22 (1981), p. 4.
3 I wish to underline that the incident shows Schoenberg's belief that
   his musical language is his personal discovery or creation. His conviction that the system was his property and could not be appropriated
   even by a fictional character shows the depth of his feeling on the
   matter.
4 Renato Poggioli, trans. Gerald Fitzgerald, *The Theory of the Avant-
   Garde* (Cambridge, Mass., 1968), p. 64.
5 Poggioli, p. 73.
6 Nicholas Kenyon, ed., Authenticity and Early Music (Oxford 1988),
   p. 152.
7 Habermas, p. 4.
8 Dover Publications (New York, 1939).
9 Allen, p. xx.
10 Allen, p. 104.
11 Allen, p. 3.
12 Allen, p. 294.
13 I am conscious of writing from the peculiar perspective of the

academic musical community, which has usually left the significance of the huge increase in popular music to one side. I am trying to describe a transformation within that tradition, which appears to be unaffected by the music of the larger culture. I am aware that there are good reasons to argue that it is here, in the sphere of popular music, where the largest proportion of music has been created in the twentieth century. However, one would still have to make an account of the music written for the concert hall throughout this period.

14 Virginia Hancock, *Brahms's Choral Compositions and his Library of Early Music* (Ann Arbor, Mich., 1983).

15 'By the time the work was complete, he had so thoroughly incorporated techniques from this study into his own style that countless examples of their use, may be found throughout it, and indeed in all of his compositions (p. 128).

16 One wonders though, how far those elements which we would recognise as historically unstylistic would be apparent to ears which had only just began to hear this music, given the willingness to adapt the music of the past to nineteenth-century taste. Hancock recounts the story of how a member of a choir was quite accepting of the explanation that Brahms was 'some old ecclesiastic of Palestrina's time', and while she thinks the singer was undoubtedly credulous, she adds 'that the idea is not quite so ludicrous in the case of the Begräbnisgesang', adding, seemingly to save Brahms from the charge of not reflecting the *Zeitgeist*, 'nevertheless the work, in innumerable details of harmony, rhythm, part writing and instrumentation, especially in the middle C major section, demonstrates Brahms as a composer of his own time' (p. 114). The point I wish to make is that given our more refined sense of historical exactitude we are able to identify nineteenth-century aspects of these pieces where those at the time would be unable to do so.

17 Hancock, p. 111.

18 Hancock, p. 116.

19 Hancock, p. 116.

20 Hancock, p. 117.

21 Hancock, p. 128.

22 Hancock, p. 128.

23 Hancock, p. 136.

24 Habermas, 'Modernity versus Postmodernity', p. 5.

25 Habermas, p. 5.

26 Habermas, p. 5.

Peter Jowers

Beating new tracks: WOMAD and the British world music movement

Introduction

In this chapter I explore the 'world music phenomenon' as it has occurred in Britain between 1981 and the present.[1] My thesis is that it is best understood as a response in the field of culture to the condition of postmodernity. It is an exemplary case of a new social movement. I commence with a brief discussion of post-modernity before discussing new social movements and their relation to this wider process. 'World music' has given rise to many vituperative arguments over its meaning and implications. I review such debates. They are a fully expected example of reflexivity. Such debates can be constitutive in that they act as self-corrections to certain courses of action. I shall then seek to confirm my thesis by focusing upon the work of WOMAD, an organisation with which I am very familiar and which I take as a typical case exemplifying my argument.[2]

On postmodernism

I identify three models of postmodernity. These are: the spectral, heroic and organic. The first and best established is derived from Jameson. The second, associated with post-Marxism, theorises late modernity. It covers similar theoretical issues. The last models subordinate tendencies within contemporary society.[3] Each assumes specific conceptual understandings of our contemporary condition and derives different ethico-political conclusions. I compare them around their different uses of the concepts of history, subjectivity and reflexivity.[4]

In most postmodern theory the two strands of Marxist and Weberian theory are variably combined with post-structuralism. The Marxist aspect leads to a focus on the radical restructuring and globalisation of late capitalism. From this are derived theories concerning the restructuring of global time and space. Various figures such as space/time 'compression', 'shrinkage' and 'collapse' are used to explore the impact of this process upon a range of social phenomena. Of primary interest has been the linkage of global media, global communications and data bases and financial markets in a climate of deregulation.[5]

The Weberian strand has emphasised an alteration in the trajectory of the rationalisation process and the accompanying differentiation of cultural spheres. Modernity was viewed as engendering a deepening of differentiation whereby different spheres of social activity separated into different 'expert' domains, 'abstract' or 'complex' systems. The religious was separated from the secular which in turn sub-divided into discrete domains: the economic, political, aesthetic, etc.[6] Each separated further and became increasingly reflexive, specialised and 'expert', based upon lengthy training and credentialisation. Rationalisation implies an ever deepening iron cage of bureaucracy and hierarchical administered social relations. It can be called a 'process of abstraction'. Much postmodern theory views this process as interrupted and partially reversed engendering movement from the grand narratives of Enlightenment rationality towards a world of difference and heterogeneity identifying a process of de-differentiation. It implies a loosening of the boundaries between expert systems, the fusion of high and low culture, etc., and a general implosion of distinct domains. A general crisis of rationality, as traditionally conceived, has been identified.[7] Organisationally this results in a move away from strict hierarchy towards more lateral 'networks'.

In the three models, I detect much overlap in the utilisation of these two streams of social theory. Interest lies in their different diagnosis of the forms and the impact of postmodernity upon personal and collective identities and the ethico-political response this implies. Understanding of world music will vary depending upon how postmodernity is modelled.

Jameson's work is the exemplary form of spectral postmodernism. He still assumes fairly traditional historical teleology and economic reductionism. Despite claiming that postmodernism is not to be conceived of as monolithic, or moralistically, and that he seeks to provide an analytical account from which 'certain aspects of postmodernism can be seen as relatively positive', in fact his model is deeply pessimistic.[8] Such positivity he finds is drawn a priori from his teleological view of history. He claims that 'The dialectic requires us to hold equally to a positive or "progressive" evaluation of its [postmodernism's] emergence'. This demands 'the invention and elaboration of an internationalism of a radically new type' and a 'pedagogical political culture which seeks to endow the individual subject with some new heightened sense of its place in the global system'.[9] This deep pessimism results from a sense of history taking the wrong direction, its inner rationality thwarted by contemporary capitalism.

In both the other models there is a decisive rejection of such foundationalism in favour of a view of history as being radically contingent. They stress the multiplicity of possible histories which can be written and a more open potential for strategic intervention both of which have important implications for analysis of world music. A univocal history is challenged to make possible multiple histories which are not part of a larger meaning of an underlying idea or force.[10] Ernesto Laclau, whose work exemplifies the heroic model, writes: 'the outcomes of ... different moments depend on contingent power relations, between forces that cannot be reduced to any kind of logic'.[11] Similarly, Melucci, whose work exemplifies the organic school, argues: 'metasocial principles, such as the Will of God or the Laws of History, are losing their grip on society. For the first time ever, society itself senses that it is contingent and in need of continuous construction'.[12]

Radical contingency does not mean that everything is experienced as contingent. We live within constructed, embedded social relations.[13] The heroic model stresses that the social is a human construction. Embedded social relations conceal their original fictive quality and conceal power. Asymmetries of power underpin discursive regimes, patterns of exploitation and domination. Their complex articulations constitute the social realm, our sense of objectivity and our relationally forged identities. Such power is naturalised, its fictive arbitrariness concealed.[14] As Laclau notes 'The system of possible alternatives tends to fade. In this way, the instituted tends to assume the form of a mere objective presence. This is the moment of *sedimentation*.'[15] Late modernity is viewed as

an intensified comprehensive questioning of such sedimentation in
the name of a continuing democratic revolution which is becoming
global. The organic model places at its heart the production of
'alternative perceptions and meanings of the world'. It insists upon
the challenge that new collectivities pose for administered complex
systems which systematically evacuate and sequester crucial ethical
and political questions. It challenges the imperatives of late modernity and offers prefigured alternatives.[16]

The most significant differences between the three models occur
in relation to notions of the subject and the interrelated topic
of identity. Each assumes that subjects are social constructions
rejecting foundational humanism. They agree that the passage to
modernity has been one in which 'traditional' social relations which
produced relatively fixed identities have progressively disembedded.
The securing of coherent identities has become problematic. The
organic model perceives strategies emerging which combat this
process. It presupposes much of the spectral model's analysis
but concentrates upon detailed examination of positive tendencies
within the present.

Key differences occur around the tropes of stability and fluidity.
The spectral model pessimistically detects little but danger in the
fluidity of the postmodern condition. Jameson mobilises an intertextual cluster of images drawn from W. B. Yeats's 'The Second
Coming' to write in high apocalyptic style on the fragmentary
quality of contemporary subjectivity making no attempt to limit
this description sociologically. He writes of 'our' condemnation
to parodic utterance, our speech in a dead language, our being
amputated of the satiric impulse and our lack of conviction. We
randomly cannibalise all the styles of the past, the subject can
produce nothing but heaps of fragments. Our cultural productions
are randomly heterogenous and aleatory. They are eclectic, they
lack coherent ordering bases and consequently 'we' live increasingly
in an aleatory world of pure chance.[17]

The consequence is a schizophrenic condition. Faced with a
breakdown of coherence the ordering principles of our personal and
collective narratives and sense of place have been shattered. We are
doomed to wander in the rubble of distinct and unrelated signifiers
increasingly shorn of any relation to referents, wolves in the ruins
of culture. Our ability to distinguish clearly between inner subjectivity and material reality is increasingly vitiated. Lacking depth,

we are increasingly driven by the primary drives of affect and emotional intensities which we affix to random signifiers torn from their referents. Hallucinating, we are traversed by alternating bouts of anxiety and euphoria.[18]

Jameson's bewilderment stems from his horror at the new globalisation; of capital, intensified media linkages and an accelerating commodification of culture. His real analytical weakness is to combine non-sociological generalisation with an underestimation of the reflexive capacities of contemporary subjects. His call for 'an aesthetic of cognitive mapping' is well known.[19] Spectral postmodernism ends in the immobilism of vague incantation. We live as fragmented shards in the placelessness of a globalised mediascape linked only via real and electronic highways.

If all is dissolution in the spectral model, for heroic modernism the problem of contemporary society is fixity. Consequently it demands emancipation 'from the fixities of tradition and from conditions of hierarchical domination'. Giddens defines such emancipatory politics as:

a generic outlook concerned above all with liberating individuals and groups from constraints which adversely affect their life chances. [It] involves . . . the effort to shed shackles of the past, thereby permitting a transformative attitude towards the future; and the aim of overcoming the illegitimate domination of some individuals or groups by others.[20]

Heroic modernism draws us back to the lived realities of many in contemporary society whose problem is not spectral dissolution, a psychic disorientation centred on images of bodily fragmentation, but real absence of basic needs and minimal life-chances.

Where spectral postmodernists sense all social bonds loosening, heroic modernists argue that a further dissolution is needed. The central problem of heroic moderns is well stated by Bennett: 'it can only be a negative oppositional politics; it lacks a conception of the positivity of the social capable of supporting forms of politics directed toward the construction of a new social order'.[21] At stake is the problem of how both to encourage emancipatory potential, to increase life chances, and yet simultaneously to find some anchors upon which to build identities and collective action not grounded either in sedimented social practice or on the basis of a retreat into foundational or escapist fundamentalisms. For heroic modernism recourse to the past, tradition and above all nostalgia is regressive, the crime of all crimes. Here lies a real problem of obvious interest to the discussion of world music. Much depends on which recourse to sources is made. Such views are locked into many unquestioned assumptions derived from Enlightenment models of autonomy and rationality. It is quite possible to generate new histories, new senses of time and place, new narratives of the previously excluded, quite self-consciously in order to build a future in which the demands of emancipation simultaneously exist with continuity, globalisation with a sense of place and community.[22] Heroic postmodernism has an unsubtle sense of the past as a nightmare to awaken from. Laclau typically argues that

a world organised round traditional social relations is one in which the possibilities of variation and transformation are strictly limited: human beings cannot choose and build their own life because it has already been organised for them by a pre-existent social system.[23]

Though one is on very poor grounds in seeking to defend tradition, heroic modernism does seem to be endlessly replaying the eighteenth-century quarrel of the ancients and moderns. We construct histories to suit our contemporary struggles. Tradition is not one vast field of similarity. The binary tropes of stasis and dynamism centred on modernity and tradition are simplistic. They elide the complex history of such societies, their interactions with modern industrial societies and the complex hybrid cultures which have emerged and continue to emerge. Heroic modernism has for too long accepted the sociological founding fathers' vision of tradition as repetitive oppressive stagnation.[24]

Melucci offers more subtlety. Fully accepting the implications of modernity, he argues that complex differentiated societies 'are unable to provide forms of membership and identification to meet individuals' needs for self-realisation, communicative interaction and recognition'. Selective de-differentiation offers the individual a partially stable identity 'via a return to primary memberships'. For example the revitalisation of ethnicity introduces new themes within older continuities, stopping such reaffirmations of ethnicity becoming 'archaic, utopian and regressive'. The ethno-national question 'contains a plurality of meanings that cannot be reduced to a single core' and can be used as a 'weapon of revenge against centuries of discrimination'. The ethnic appeal launches its chal-

lenge to complex society on such fundamental questions as the
goals of change and the production of identity and meaning. 'Difference is thereby given a voice which speaks of problems which
traverse the whole of society'.[25] Other collectivities centred on
gender, sexual preference, ecology, etc. offer similar needs for
recognition. Communities are linked sets of mutual recognitions.

Organic postmodernism offers another view of our present condition. Lash writes that the 'organic critique of modernity is associated with ecological, communitarian and localist social movements
and is often *not considered to be postmodern in conventional parlance*'
(my emphasis). It breaks with high modernism, it seeks to de-
differentiate and break with 'reason which is not socially situated'.
If spectral postmodernism is imploded into the mediascape, the
organic seeks a rationality which is socially situated where culture is
reappropriated. It allows for 'genuine difference of particularised
communities' from which a 'situational ethics' can be derived.[26]

This model, when fleshed out with new social movement theory,
holds the key to understanding much of the world music phenomenon. Giddens analyses in depth the condition of the self in late
modernity. Shorn of sedimented supports, identities have to be
continually constructed. Reflexivity is the key concept here. Defined
as choice in the face of an indefinite range of potential courses of
action with attendant risks, it implies choosing between counterfactual 'possible worlds'. These have to be imagined prior to their
possible consideration. Recourse to sources is merely one way to
imagine them. Reflexivity entails an orientation to the future,
generation of counterfactual possibilities and evaluation of the risk
in realising them.[27]

Reflexivity entails recognition 'that the ends, means, conditions
and legitimations of any given action in which one is involved are
not the only ones possible'.[28] If reference points evaporate, then
mobile or nomadic identity coupled with continuous and reflexive
metamorphosis becomes the best response.

Melucci explains the turn to 'intensities' decried by the spectral
model as an escape from instrumental rationality in an attempt to
ground subjectivity in the use of 'more immediate perceptions,
intuitive awareness and imagination that were *the patrimony of
traditional cultures*' (my emphasis). This turn is a symptom of
individuals' need to unify experience beyond mere rational and
instrumental thought.[29]

Identifying this turn to intensities is useful in understanding one facet of world music. Middleton argues that 'music is the primary metaphor' because its origins lie in the aural relationship of 'baby and mother', which, together with the tactile, pre-dates the 'significance of visual (still more, verbal) signs'. The repetitive sound of maternal breathing and the heartbeat 'are prior to any emergence of the subject'. On such a reading the unconscious is structured like music. Middleton stresses an opposition between 'traditional European song forms' which are syntactical, analogue and hierarchically based, with 'Afro-American Forms' which use a binary form of repetition. Andrew Chester pursues a similar argument by contrasting the extensional development of classical music with the intentional form of rock music founded on the 'inflection of the basic beat'. While the binary/hierarchical opposition can be accepted, the geography and racial stereotyping cannot be. Phillip Tagg has demolished such polarities once and for all. This return to intensities Lash describes as 'the return of desire' which 'as a renunciation of signification . . . asks not what a cultural text means but what it does'. He explains this as 'the extension of the primary process, in Freudian terms into the cultural realm . . . [which] operates through the "spectator's" [sic] investment of his/her desire in the cultural object'. Postmodern theorists' obsession with the figural could be challenged from this aural stance.[30]

Such observations help to explain the curious amalgam which forms the world music mix, its Afrocentrism and clustering around the binary repetitive pole, whether in the form of traditional Gaelic, Balkan or other 'roots' musics, and its overlap with other contemporary musics such as House, etc. Much of the content of world music radio programmes and festivals can then be understood.

Reflexivity applies to individuals, collectivities and institutions. Subjectivity depends upon recognition; identity cannot be conceived of as other than inter-subjective. The nightmare of spectral postmodernism is a picture of an imploding mediascape with no mutuality, isolation within mere empty signs. New social movements are mutual support systems grounded in the life-world rather than in bureaucratic administration. They seek to enhance mutuality and solidarity while simultaneously transforming the social imaginary. If reflexivity implies an acceptance of risks, only relatively 'secure' individuals can take risks. Such security is founded upon trust, upon partially predictable intersubjectivity. New social movements consequently use much of their time and resources sustaining themselves as frameworks of trust.[31] On the ground of trust a sense of a shared reality of self, other persons and things can be constructed. Paranoid space need not be defended, schizophrenia can be avoided. Defensive constructions of identity founded upon lack of trust solidify into escapist fundamentalisms coupled with unintegrated intensities of anxiety and euphoria. In contrast open reflexively grounded identity accepts fluidity, integrates primary processes into a sustained, coherent and yet continuously revised biographical narrative. Pathologies arise from obstacles to this conscious production of one's identity which can be no other than simultaneously social.[32]

Recognition of the crucial role of biographical narrative in the construction of coherent identity can be broadened out to encompass shared narratives of collectivities. History returns but this time not as nostalgia and refuge but as a ground, as reflexively constructed continuity between past, present and reflexively debated images of the future. It is a writing in the extended sense, of a shared journey, not a visit to a commodified past of 'heritage' predigested for non-reflexive nostalgia or behind the barricades of fundamentalisms. Mutuality may be 'placed', associated with territory, but this is not necessary.

Many aspect of new social theory cannot be dealt with here. The movements it discusses have the following characteristics. They have unstable patterns of memberships. They operate within a set of structural constraints and opportunities, take plural forms, conflict is less about resources and more about challenging formal, rational existing frameworks of knowledge. They challenge the existing codes upon which social relationships are founded and reveal their irrationality and bias. Such organisations are self-reflexive in that they continuously monitor their own ends and means. Their external objectives are not separate from their internal forms.

Such movements seek to generate new meanings in order to stimulate ethical and political questioning concerning issues hidden, submerged or sequestered from public view by the existing administered systems of politics. They seek to create public spaces in which responsibility for the goals of social life can be debated. As Melucci writes, they 'take the form of networks . . . which act as cultural laboratories. They require individual investments in the experimentation and practice of new cultural models, forms of relationships and alternative perceptions and meanings of the world.'[33] To innovate culturally and generate new meanings, existing cultural elements have to be gathered and reordered. Innovation goes by way of a 'rag-bag of existing cultural elements' until such time as a new form of reality crystallises and more appropriate cultural codes are discovered. This recycling of elements helps to clarify eclecticism much derided in the spectral model from innovative hybridity.

Hybridity is a creative response to social change which has a unifying thrust but, because it seeks the new within the older codes, has to twist and warp meaning through numerous strategies to simultaneously distance, deconstruct and disrupt established usage while by juxtaposition, fusion, grafting and numerous other rhetorical strategies hinting at the new.[34]

The task of new collectivities is to engender new spaces and sites for coherent identity formation, to question how we should live our lives in emancipated social circumstances and remoralise a vitiated institutionally repressed social life.[35] In seeking to achieve this in their various domains, they make use of the full panoply of existing semiotic society. As challengers of cultural codes they are reflexively sophisticated about the meaning and uses of signs which operate at the heart of contemporary media and provide many of the new cohorts entering the culture industries. New social movements fade one from another in the sense that individuals may be active in more than one movement. The world music movement draws upon its linkages with more enduring movements, such as Anti-Apartheid, etc.

If heroic modernism concentrates upon a necessary negation of existing embedded oppressions and denials of life-chances, spectral postmodernism successfully warns of tendential dangers of our contemporary condition; only organic postmodernism offers concrete strategic action and guides to concrete utopias which in turn must be continually renegotiated.

The rise of world music in Britain

Here I briefly trace the genealogy of the term 'world music'. It emerged later than the activities with which it has been subsequently associated.[36] Once it appeared, tied to a sustained and planned marketing campaign, the implicit reflexivity which had accompanied these activities stimulated an extremely sustained bout of writing and theorising.

Those bringing such diverse musicians to Britain or releasing records or playing such music on radio had been casting around for a term to describe what they were doing. From 1982 the term 'world beat' was being bandied about.[37] In a British context it seemed stilted. The only other available terms seemingly available were 'third world music' and 'ethnic music', appalling in their Eurocentric condescension. For example, some unnamed reviewer of the first WOMAD festival in 1982 wrote: 'I passed some time roaming around with my colleagues discussing the validity of showing these assorted *'ethnic'* musics out of context, arbitrarily selected (unlike most multi-national arts fests) by a rock sensibility'.[38] Mark Kidel wrote of the same festival about 'the combination of "*ethnic musics with popular groups*"', while John Haywood used a more neutral description of *'foreign styles'* and 'an aurally eclectic weekend'.[39] Charles de Ledesma, reviewing another WOMAD festival, this time at Mersea in Essex in 1985, wrote of it being 'a musical journey through some of the world's unrecorded "*musica folklorique*"'.[40] By a year later, 1986, Philip Sweeney was writing: 'Musicologists . . . could ponder . . . the growing politicisation and internationalism of all "*Third* World Music"'.[41] The first actual use that I have found of 'world music' as a discrete signifier of this growing plethora of activity came in an article in *Folk Roots* in September 1985. Dave Amoros described the Mersea festival of 1985 as a 'dazzling display of *world music* [with] just the right amount of interesting UK rock to keep the punters coming'.[42] While it is clear that the new term was emerging, other descriptions persisted. Graham Evans reviewing WOMAD's 1986 festival, wrote of it as 'a forum for the best in *world music*',[43] in the same period *Music Week* was using the term *'global jukebox'*.[44]

1987 was the *annus mirabilis* for 'world music'. The concept began to crop up more frequently in *Folk Roots*, the leading magazine dealing with this music.[45] The crucial determining event was in the late autumn of that year when representatives from eleven independent record labels and key organisations such as WOMAD and World Circuit and Folk Roots met in The King of Prussia, a London pub, to thrash out a joint marketing concept around the chosen term 'world music'. Though others were invited, those present decided the issue. Following this meeting a joint advertisement appeared in *Folk Roots* in its December 1987 edition. This definition by fiat engendered considerable early hostility from those hostile to the music, those associated with it who disliked the term, and those who felt left out.[46]

From the spring of 1988 the rush was on. 'World music, was a godsend to record companies, promoters, agencies, journalists, TV and radio producers, festival organisers, educationalists, the state and local state sponsors and of course to artists themselves. The process peaked in the two years which followed. By the end of 1990, its impetus in Britain had rapidly waned. World music sections of music stores had been withdrawn or considerably scaled down, world music records were remaindered, record releases were at an all-time low, funding was difficult to obtain. The impact of the poll tax and rate capping and the general deepening of recession had all taken their toll. Many locally based promoters had taken a financial pasting and, if dependent upon sponsored support, had seen their grants declining fast.[47]

From a nadir in mid-1991 there has been a revival in the British fortunes of world music. In one sense this difficult period has resulted in a shake-out of the less professional parts of the network. WOMAD has regained much confidence with the success of its innovative recording week of August 1991 which involved the collaboration of over sixty musicians from all over the world coupled with top-class producers all taking place at Peter Gabriel's Real World Studios. This event, a type of creative risk with expensive studio time, resulted in extensive media coverage, two hour-long broadcasts by the BBC which financially underwrote the event and, at the time of writing, four albums already released with more to follow. The impact of the event both within the narrow compass of the professional music industry and on the public interested in such music has been considerable. The event is to be repeated in August 1992, this time funded by two day-long festivals in Bath with anticipated audiences of ten thousand. Given the impact of such media exposure, a new audience seems to have been reached. The 1992 Reading festival was full to capacity. The general sense of well-being and continued activity has been reflected in the pages of *Folk Roots*, though ignored by the mainstream musical newspapers.

Boom and near bust and then stabilisation: is this how we should

view the British world music phenomenon? The general consensus
is that world music is not destined to be as important as it once
appeared likely to become, but is settling into a gently expanding
niche in the musical field rather akin to the blues and jazz. Despite
much disappointment by many in the network this seems entirely
predictable given the social basis of its support in Britain. The UK
is still a crucial nodal point in the global popular music industry,
particularly in innovation and style-setting. The definition of world
music and its rapid growth stimulated much interest elsewhere
in Europe, with only France and Holland following relatively independent courses as a result of their links with previous colonies.
Their independent nexus stimulated much futile debate as to where
the centre of world music was to be located.[48]

Debating the meaning of world music

Goodwin and Gore define 'world beat' as Western pop stars ap-
propriating non-Western sounds, as third world musicians using
Western rock and pop, or as the Western consumption of non-
Western folk music.[49] The short and intensive debate concerning
the meaning of 'world music' commenced in early 1988 and
culminated in the autumn of 1989. Current debate merely rakes
over the coals wondering why what seemed 'the next big thing in
music' never really happened. The earlier reflexive moment dealt in
rather abstract, large-scale issues conjoined with much vituperative
point-scoring and posturing. Space precludes detailed discussion.[50]

Band Aid and *Graceland* triggered off a probably familiar debate
which needs no repetition here.[51] Goodwin and Gore pose one facet
of importance. Is the world music phenomenon to be viewed
optimistically as a 'progressive intervention within Western culture'
or is it a classic example of 'old forms of exploitation and cultural
imperialism'? The first stance they find too naive, despite the fact
that such music 'suggests an element of feed back in the one way
flow which has often characterised global communications' and the
second too pessimistic. They stress that much of the flow of profit
from such music goes to the multinational record companies. This
point is reiterated by Glanville.[52]

The world music scene abounds with tales of 'rip-offs' like the
rock world. Glanville notes the desperate desire of many musicians
who wish to play in the West in their 'willingness to pitch at the

"European and North American market"'. On tour with Nusrat Fateh Ali Khan I found the band astounded that the local promoter to whom the tour had been sub-contracted in Germany had issued a record of Nusrat's of which they had absolutely no knowledge. It transpired that it was an old recording for which they had, as is usual, taken a flat-rate cash fee, the only protection in Pakistan in the absence of any legal enforcement of contracts. The local German promoter had licensed this recording in all good faith. Nusrat's solution has been to build his own studio, which nears completion. Many of the bands I have toured with are extremely interested in acquiring technology and equipment to enhance their power 'back home', something which WOMAD seeks to encourage.

Glanville notes the lack of unity among musicians even to the extent of internally exploitative relationships within bands. There have been notorious cases of tours which have collapsed because of such internal strains. His plea 'that it is time the musicians showed some unity, fought for what is justly theirs and took control in the way in which Western artists are learning to do' is crucial advice. Given the huge and shifting numbers of musicians from all parts of the world and the number of companies and agencies involved this is a very uphill task, though the internal grapevine within the world music community does act as a regulating mechanism and artists and their management who meet at festivals and gigs pay careful attention to standards and track-records of various companies. The more successful artists quickly learn as they travel increasingly and with both the export of technology and experience are better able to advise those embarking on a similar journey and to take increasing control over their own recordings. Such transfers build upon their ability to earn income abroad, something which the world music phenomenon has facilitated. Access to sophisticated engineering and studio technologies enables them to aspire to the highest international standards.

Much debate has occurred concerning the role of European-based production values. There have been several appalling examples where production techniques applicable to European sensibilities have been foisted upon musicians unfamiliar with the technology and in a very dependent position vis-à-vis their record company or sponsors. It is of vital importance that such engineering and acoustic skills should be transferred along with the necessary equipment. This is beginning to happen. A danger is that only certain élite acts will benefit, further enhancing their power in their own regions. The uses such facilities are put to is quite correctly beyond the control of those involved with world music in the West. Musicians are fully aware of these issues. Baaba Maal argues for instance:

I know there are many African musicians who are frustrated because they can't use *African* instruments on stage. . . . So Africans have to search for ways to match modern technology with the needs of African instruments, retaining the same acoustic qualities. . . . The problem we have in Senegal is a shortage of engineers rather than of instruments. Finding a way to record the voice, and certain African instruments, how to capture those sounds, those possibilities. For the moment we still haven't found all the answers.[53]

Much of the debate concerns not the specifics of economic control but the manner in which music is consumed and used. Much of contemporary cultural studies seeks to find points of resistance within commercialised forms of popular culture. The key issue here in relation to the consumption of world music in the West is exactly by whom and how it is received. Here a cluster of criticisms have been made.

Key areas of debate centred on whether 'world music' entailed anything of substance. Many of the vituperative contributions seemed bent on criticising the possibility of any creative inter-cultural communication which did not fall back into either old forms of cultural imperialism or mere consumption of the other as exotic titivation for jaded musical palettes, the equivalent of post-modern lifestyle consumption without depth. Much of the response seemed to imply that involvement in the music could take place only by way of pre-existent categories of consumption. It has been noted again and again that much of what passes for world music consists of African dance music or musics which are compatible with Western definitions of music. There is considerable pressure here from the public. It is quite clear to me, as an active promoter of such music for many years, that there is an obvious audience for electric African music as there is, somewhat surprisingly, for for 'exotic' colourful dance acts such as The Tibetan Institute for Performing Arts or the Cambodian National Dance. It is virtually impossible to raise an audience for quiet contemplative acoustic music of any complexity in a musicological sense.

There is much talk of world music as 'aural tourism', of the 'music industry . . . exploiting the exoticism of far away places' and the promotion of a bogus one-worldism to sell such music.[54] As Oldfield and Reynolds argue, 'in fact world music's devotees scarcely discover anything unfamiliar in other cultures. Instead they've created this "world" to staunch the crisis of faith in our pop and have grafted their own very Western, very 80's preoccupations on to it.' They discover that one group finds 'maturity, sophistication, open-mindedness and cosmopolitan cool' in world music whilst the other finds 'rock-like rootsiness (hence the Afrocentrism of so-called "world" music sponteneism and honesty)'. Each group is attracted to the other because they are both disillusioned with their own societies in crisis and project on to other cultures 'a vicarious sense of belonging, of community, *wherever* it's to be found'. The other is seen to represent the 'authenticity and ruralness that the Western world has forfeited'. Often tagged on to this line of criticism is the notion of world music as mere fad. In a very incoherent conclusion, they argue that this desire for 'authenticity' ignores the repressive nature of all society and that if such cultures 'seem balanced, they don't have the ills of deviance, dissent and decadence that we suffer, that's because they've never aquired the models of individual *freedom* and growth, self-expression or naturalness that we are so eager to attribute to them'. In seeking to protect them from the homogen-ising effects of the West, and in adopting spurious one-worldism, the 'we are all brothers under the skin syndrome', we are in effect practising ideological colonialism. In consequence because of our preoccupations we do not hear their irreducible otherness, we are force-feeding them our ideology of heritage just as we once fed them modernity and development. 'We've made our culture into a theme park; they must do the same.' By seeking to restore self-respect, self-determination and traditions of other cultures we are 'simply teaching them liberal values annexing them further into our ways of thinking'. Instead of being caring colonialists by listening to other musics, we should 'forget Africa', we should submit to the irreducible otherness of music that is still a dark continent which is a trip out of this world 'not a detour back to our own enlightened values'.[55]

At issue here is a technical point of 'translation' or a hermeneutic issue. Without pre-existing musical categories the musical other would appear utterly unknowable. Is it surprising then that, in commencing an exploration of other musics, more assimilable forms would gain acceptance first and more opaque ones later? I detect such a pattern. Given the rhythms of West African music in particular, which were soon followed by an increasing awareness of the huge range and variety of African musics in general, I find it no surprise that this should have remained the most consistently popular entry point for many into 'world music'. Particularly younger members of the world music community were attracted to the sheer danceability of the music. Such criticism of large numbers of people who were actively involved in the Anti-Apartheid struggle, of those who had worked in Africa in the 'aid and development' field who saw the music as a way of passing on their enthusiasm and concerns for a wider range of issues, or who had travelled there, such simple denigration is callow and simplistic.

All translation must begin somewhere. Assimilation into an existing framework is only a primary phase. Interest in such musics becomes increasingly reflexive. The ability to absorb other musical forms develops as understanding of their complexity deepens, enabling an intensifying appreciation of the diversity and depth of other musical cultures to grow which simultaneously calls into question the dispersion and valorisation of Western musical fields. It is no surprise that hand in hand with the emergence of world music has gone an intensifying interest in European traditional music which has been re-evaluated in relation to classical and other forms and in Britain rescued from the dead hand of the 'folk' fraternity.

Given the vast range of possible musics there is a tendency for 'area specialisations' to emerge. While some continue to explore African music, others consolidate their interest in Latin, North African, Arabic, Eastern European musics, etc. Often such interests are determined by existing contacts, linguistic abilities or undefinable affinities. In an increasingly multi-cultural Britain diverse ethnic groups and particularly second generation citizens have found 'world music' a way of communicating their difference to a wider British audience and in turn have been attracted to other musics expressive of similar experiences here. To travel as tour manager with say a Zambian, Egyptian or Pakistani group is to be constantly astounded at the sheer numbers, cultural complexity and isolation of many of these people who find immense pride in reaffirming their identity via performances and in sharing it with others.

One important index of this growing reflexivity has been the impact of world music on adjacent musical genres within the over-all field of music-making and consumption. The influx of new sounds has been profound, including a revitalisation of the rhythmic components of much of British and European jazz, and a revitalisation of European 'traditional' musics with subtle uses of elements from Eastern Europe and Africa, as in Irish music for example. WOMAD has been immensely influential in the Bristol area's music in this respect. The widening use of sampling has enabled these textures to penetrate many facets of rock music and House music and in turn has strengthened the hybridisation of indigenous immigrant musics. Without 'world music' neither the music-makers nor their audience could have explored this dynamic and fertile field of musical innovation so easily or with such vigour. Increasingly, as the WOMAD recording week and the 1992 Reading festival made clear, a uniquely new type of music is in the making. It is hybrid in the sense that those from one musical tradition are incorporating elements from other traditions without lapsing into mere eclecticism.

On this view involvement in such musics becomes a deepening affair in which a hermeneutic 'fusion of horizons' grows and develops from which interest in music broadens out into an exploration of an area's history and its wider culture. In turn this brings a critical attention to contemporary political and economic issues and to the role of the West in sustaining exploitation. I do not claim that this pattern is necessary, merely that it is common. It may explain why world music was never destined to become more than a specialised field within musical consumption in general, attracting an interest from a particular and critical segment of contemporary society typical of those involved in the new social movements. Further, as this type of involvement grows, the need for an overarching label of 'world music' becomes increasingly redundant and banal, though it has served a useful mediating role in gaining media attention and acceptability. World music may have temporarily attracted the fickle followers of musical fashions as exemplified by the brief flirtations with it of *The New Musical Express* and *Q* which have since ceased but it has established an audience of its own which has now stabilised and will probably expand, if at all, very slowly.[56]

The charge of searching for 'roots', for 'authenticity', in short a latter-day Romanticism, underestimates the sophistication of the audience. Such aspects of cultural interaction do have an attraction, and can be used as a critique of 'modern abstraction'. There is no naive view of the conditions from which the music arises. There is real recognition of the urbanisation and social upheavals engendering the hybridity of music from the 'south'. Such difference, founded upon an awareness of contemporary reality, must refract back upon our own assumptions. This means that exploitation within the 'south' by Western-sponsored élites, ancient patriarchy, racial oppression and regressive fundamentalisms is not ignored. Nevertheless, as the Rushdie affair taught us, the cardinal rule of our postmodern era is that we can no longer uncritically accept our own dogmas of modernity as foundational. Just as hybrid music has appeared, so too, through the opening of a space for fusions of horizons – while simultaneously acknowledging the innumerable asymmetries of power this often entails – ethical hybridity may emerge. A flourishing debate and reflexive communication from within 'difference' has been opened up. World music has made its small contribution to the emergence of a form of global civil society from which an emerging ethics might be translated into effective political analysis and action to address those blatant oppressions and crises which afflict us all. I choose to finish this section with Baaba Maal whose views better capture my intuitions concerning such music than the jaded cynicism of Oldfield and Reynolds. He observes:

People want to come together, they want to know one another, and with that we can sort out a lot of things – racism, egotism. It is important that people make those openings, and get to know one another, and through that we can arrive at tolerance . . . I'm confident that music will play an important part in creating that rapprochement between people, where ever they are.[57]

WOMAD and the world music network

WOMAD's legitimacy derives from its being the first coherent focus for the emerging world music movement. This movement exemplifies a network structure as predicted by new social movement theory. Networks are non-hierarchical, display multiple leadership, and entail temporary ad hoc organisational structures founded upon variable individual commitments. Any organisations which emerge alter according to the learning process of its acting members.[58] Each node of a network (individual, group or organisation) makes its own decisions, and communication flows from node to node in any direction. Networks do not conform to top-down hierarchical forms. Densities of interaction make key areas of networks more central. Where activities, information flows, experiential and financial resources are at their most clustered, new élites emerge who are crucial to the functioning of the network as a whole. The network as a whole monitors performance. Key individuals and organisations emerge who, in the reflexive learning process, have garnered the most experience, have perhaps been the most innovative or the most reliable and most fair to the competing interests with which they have been involved.

Given a media-saturated society, those with access to, who are inside, influential media or who create new information poles have considerable authority. Definitions and debates of the movement as a whole tend to be played out by such élites. In the world music movement this is not often explicit, but it is exemplified more in choices of performers, recordings, areas of music, organisational innovation, forms of presentation, treatment of artists, etc. If such influence becomes unacceptable it results in these persons or organisations being bypassed and the flows within the network being re-ordered. As a consequence participation entails high levels of anxiety and stress, as 'network access' is only as good as recent involvement and performance. As a consequence elements of routinisation occur with experience. Friendships, trusted contacts, implicit rules and understandings, legitimacy founded on past performance, all emerge. Organisations which persist are forced to 'professionalise' and adopt some of the standard procedures for effective action of more normal administrative systems. This often causes points of crisis. This is the focus of my discussion of WOMAD. As a result, entry and exit are common, argument and conflict unavoidable. Performance and 'delivering the goods', such as acceptable behaviour, commitment, resources and effective action, determine access to wider areas of the network. In this manner networks can become internally self-monitoring although the conventions and rules governing these processes are rarely explicit. A situational ethics concerned with a wide range of broad issues, as well as very specific ones, emerges.

Networks do not work in a vacuum. Emerging organisations within networks 'interface' with many traditional organisations and élites such as banks, funding bodies of the local and central state, arts organisations, media and so on, and must at times conform to the rules governing their procedures, particularly if resource issues are being negotiated. This again causes controversy. Élites can shift between these areas in both directions though in the case of world music it is usually from the network into the more formal systems. In the process networks of personal contact can be maintained and trojan horses placed within the broader structures of society, fulfilling the wider reflexive role of social movements in contemporary society.

The world music network also interacts with other comparable networks. Social movements are layered. I would contend that they contain broad degrees of overlap in their membership and that while it is possible to speak of, say, the women's movement, the green movement, etc., as the theory usually does, this is a hypostatisation. These are only broad labels for an enormous range of subordinate networks often only tenuously linked. It is on this second layer that I would locate world music and within it WOMAD.

If, as the theory predicts, a social movement seeks to unearth the sequestered and concealed ethico-political dimensions of contemporary society, attempts to debate them and searches for pre-figured alternatives, then world music focuses upon the following themes. First and foremost is the aim of resisting racism and pointing to ways in which a genuine multicultural society can be pre-figured. Linked to these ends is the attempt to encourage cultural difference and heterogeneity by opening up channels of communication from the 'south' into the heartlands of the West.[59] It attempts to engage in genuine intercultural communication despite the immense difficulties this poses in conditions of asymmetrical power and resources, seemingly incommensurable difference, and an absence of common frameworks. By so doing it sets up counterfactual possibilities, making possible a form of what Verhelst calls 'Third World aid to the West'.[60] It seeks to encourage a deepening knowledge of the south in all its dimensions of hope and despair. It encourages listening in order to expand musical horizons, and to enable hybridity to emerge which links musical forms in new and imaginative ways which allow those disadvantaged to have access to Western technology and resources if they so desire. Music is not fetishised as a separate component of culture, cultures are recognised as complex formations with embedded conflict, nor is music necessarily seen as their only or even most important dimension. Finally, world music seeks to embody in its procedures partially pre-figured internal practices of mutuality and trust grounded in pleasure, which will always fall short in reality but which act as a regulative ideal. At times it is explicitly political in its anti-racism, its support for Anti-Apartheid, its resistance to government policies over Cambodia and so on but in general it engages in a form of politics, which as Derrida once put it, 'does not recognise the usual signposts'. As such it is about rewiring the codes and embedded fictions of Western cultural superiority which underpin contemporary society.

WOMAD is a key nodal point within a network of artists and performers, agencies, small and larger recording companies, arts organisations, promotors, key media personnel, educationalists and so on. It is not the only one. Those clustered around London and centred on World Circuit, the magazine *Folk Roots*, various independent record labels and radio programmes, represent another major and competing pole. The key to understanding WOMAD is to grasp how it links into the overall network and simultaneously how it straddles a very difficult path between realisation of the goals noted above of the movement in general and financial reality. Commerce and idealism intersect and the consequences are not always pretty.

WOMAD

WOMAD was born in 1982 in a baptism of fire which has haunted it since its inception. As is well known, it emerged from a chance meeting between Peter Gabriel and two young ex-university students who were in a Bristol punk band and were attempting to start a magazine, *The Bristol Recorder*, amalgamating text and local recordings. From this emerged the first WOMAD festival at Shepton Mallet. It was a financial disaster because there was no public ready for such music, and because of poor publicity, the

pulling out of BBC TV Arena's financial backing and the effects
of a rail strike.[61] The debts were paid off by Gabriel reforming
Genesis for a one-off concert in October 1982. The original WOMAD
company went into voluntary liquidation. Of interest was the fact
that an educational resource was published simultaneously with the
festival, made possible by a grant from the Commission For Racial
Equality which was distributed to Avon and Somerset schools. As a
result seven thousand children attended and participated in the
festival children's day. Also at this early stage artists brought to the
UK for the festival were booked out for appearances at other
venues. For instance The Drummers of Burundi appeared at the
Brixton Academy and the Commonwealth Institute prior to the
festival. Also a double album was compiled and released featuring
traditional and contemporary music from Africa, Asia, Latin
America and the Far East alongside contributions from well-known
Western artists.

The festival presented over three hundred artists from twenty-
eight countries, and was an artistic triumph. Like many subsequent
festivals it was staffed and run by enthusiastic volunteers many
of whom continue to belong to what could loosely be called a
WOMAD community, though since then many have left because
of disagreement over policy, unprofessional behaviour or sheer
personal differences. This first festival already revealed many of the
activities WOMAD was to be associated with in subsequent years.
Perhaps these are best summarised as: being a festival-promoting
organisation; acting as an agency; a commitment to education
through music; attempts to underwrite activities by tying into TV
and media payments; acting as a record company; negotiation with
state and local funding bodies for financial support; encouraging
collaboration between musicians from diverse backgrounds; and
acting both as an example and as a practical training ground for
those wishing to promote this type of music. WOMAD was for
many years to promote one-off gigs in Bristol. A final strand of
WOMAD activity was to emerge a year later after a two-week
'WOMAD at the ICA' was held in summer 1983. This was merch-
andise, in this case T-shirts, which were used to research and fund
the setting-up of a renewed WOMAD, this time as an educational
charity with a small administrative base in Bristol, helped in part
by *Venue*, a Bristol-based listing magazine, itself now a commercial

success, and friends in *Nova*, a commercially successful organic wholefood co-operative.[62]

In what follows I choose to concentrate only on three aspects of this plethora of activities. These are festivals, the development of the WOMAD agency and the internal organisational pressures these two facets gave rise to and which have altered again and again the trajectory that WOMAD as a whole has taken.

In many senses the history of WOMAD has been the exploration of these themes at different times with changing emphasis on the various facets coupled with growing experience and constant reflection on errors and mistakes. What began as an idealistic venture run on virtually no money, with most employees on social security or funded by MSC community programmes, has now become a sophisticated fully incorporated business in which salaries are paid and which has stringent requirements for profitability. It is this journey, in my view necessary, which estranged many people on the way, as the very success of the organisation has also done. Errors of judgement at certain times have contributed to this as has friendly and not so friendly rivalry with other nodes of the world music network. On the other hand WOMAD commands an enormous amount of credibility, good will and important linkages into the media and the complex world of agencies, managers, governments and funding sources which lie behind the surface of world music promotion and where the real skills of organisation and knowledge lie. Increasingly such skills and knowledge occur on a worldwide basis, and with growing prestige WOMAD attracts enormous numbers of artists. WOMAD is simply awash with tapes, CDs and records from musicians around the world wishing to play at its festivals, an important source of credibility and promotional material for their careers as artists.

After the disaster of 1982 it is worth noting that Peter Gabriel has taken a distant role in WOMAD's day-to-day running. He did appear at one festival prior to the Amnesty tour; in February 1989 the organisation moved to accommodation owned by Gabriel in Wiltshire after having been in Bristol for many years and entered into joint ownership of the WOMAD/Real World record label with him and Virgin Records, themselves recently part bought out by a Japanese company. Access to Gabriel's Real World studios is an important part of the Real World/WOMAD axis, enabling the finest facilities to be placed at the disposal of chosen musicians while simultaneously making available to Peter Gabriel those same musicians for projects such as *Passion* and *Passion Sources*, the music for the Martin Scorcese film *The Last Temptation of Christ*. The public perception of his close involvement has been misplaced, though his ethical influence and support during times of crisis has been important. Recently his direct involvement through the recording weeks and recording his own 1992 album and his public appearances at WOMAD festivals mark a relationship closer than in the past.

After a successful one-day festival in Bristol in 1984 financed by an independently produced and distributed compilation record accompanied by schools workshops, planning proceeded for the *Talking Book* series of records which helped to establish world music in its early form in Britain. WOMAD returned to festival promotion on the large scale in collaboration with Essex County Council at their international youth camp on Mersea Island, Essex. This festival was interesting in that it again was a financial failure, putting pressure on a newly formed company, WOMAD Festivals Ltd, despite attendances of six thousand people. As at earlier festivals and the one a year later at Clevedon just south of Bristol, several aspects were combined: firstly, performers brought in from around the world, many via government-sponsored tours; secondly, the best of newly emerging independent bands (The Pogues and New Order among others appeared there); thirdly, a strand of 'experimental' or advanced music which at this festival included The Penguin Cafe Orchestra and Jan Gabarek; and finally, many unknown and long-forgotten Bristol-based bands. This combination (which included another long-standing strand, reggae and Caribbean music, this time in the form of Toots and the Maytells) altered in two significant aspects in subsequent years. A year later, because a band on tour with a large enough rig for an outdoor festival was needed, Siouxie and the Banshees were headliners. Thomas Brooman, co-founder and director of WOMAD, put the issue squarely in a subsequent interview.

In 1986 we booked Siouxie and the Banshees and it finally felt like they were the fish out of the water – although ostensibly they were the headline band. It created tension for them and us. There was one operation going, and here was one little bit of it demanding to be treated in a different way . . . insisting that it still be rock and roll land. And the audience made it perfectly clear that they were less impressed with that rock and roll entity than with Youssou N'Dour, who preceded them on stage. This rock and roll mentality coming out helped us make a conscious decision to move away from that. . . . It's not the rock and roll ethic of endless riders and binging, but a human event of people looking after people.[63]

After 1986 the felt need to combine rock music and world music declined. An audience in its own right had been found. WOMAD continues to encourage local musicians wherever it participates in festivals, though it made a grievous error during its first venture into Barcelona in 1989 where in combination with a large financial loss it failed to book many local Catalan acts and ran into double criticism backed by the passion of Spanish regional politics.

At Clevedon in 1986 a second lesson was learnt which has shaped WOMAD festivals ever since. Firstly, the complex negotiations to hold the event were touch and go until right up to the event. Obtaining planning permission while all the arrangements for artists have to be made months in advance is no way to secure peace of mind. Secondly, despite 11,500 paying visitors the festival again lost money. Thirdly, innumerable security problems surfaced – this was the year of the first great convoy hunt through southern England. After this ordeal, despite the great success of the festival, it was decided to wind up WOMAD Festivals Ltd, to withdraw from this type of event and to seek instead forms of co-promotion as the financial context for future festivals. This model has continued ever since. By 1987 the pace was hotting up. WOMAD had its own festival within a festival at the Glastonbury Festival, at Peter Gabriel's Earls Court concerts, at Jubilee Gardens on the South Bank and most importantly a jointly promoted festival took place at The Cornwall Coliseum, Carlyon Bay, with Coliseum owners Cornish Leisure World. The new model was in place and working, for the most part well. Budgets could be well worked out, risk was spread and stability had been achieved. By having several big events in one summer bands could travel to Britain, tour and reappear at the various festivals.

In subsequent years WOMAD went international, providing festivals within festivals at Roskilde, Denmark and the Harbourfront, in Toronto, in 1988 and then spreading like wildfire in 1989 to France, Spain, Italy, Germany and Finland and from 1990 even further afield to include Japan and Australia with small groups of artists appearing at many festivals throughout Europe. These events were also locked into festivals in England, Carlyon Bay continuing in 1988 with the addition of Southhill Park, Bracknell for two years. English festivals then shifted to Morecambe in 1989 and subsequently, and Reading from 1990. In both these latter instances funding guarantees were received from local councils and various bodies such as the Arts Council, Visiting Arts and regional arts bodies. Sponsorship is also sought, being obtained from time to time from STA, a travel company, beer companies, Maxwell's ill-fated *World Beat* magazine *The Independent* newspaper and others.

Festivals entail enormous planning. In addition WOMAD had to develop expertise in very new areas. Sound engineers had to learn the music, catering and accommodation became the focus of intense internal debate as those involved with touring the various artists understood much more closely musicians' needs, which did not always mesh into festival planning. Scarred as it was by its early financial crises, treatment of artists was not always felt by the touring arm of WOMAD to be up the requisite standard. This has subsequently been resolved. In a sense the whole process – involving stage management, sound, lighting, aesthetic design and festival decoration, artists' support, workshop and children's activities, site arrangements such as services, security, tour management, publicity, media presentation and press conferences, tie-in film and video rights, acquisition of relevant visas, work permits, tax forms (the government helpfully levied a foreign entertainers' tax from 1988 of 25 per cent of gross receipts), negotiations with co-promoters, agents and managers, to mention but a few activities – meant a rise in complexity, and very rapid learning curves for those involved. They form a wide and extensive mobile community.

Festivals and touring entail real intercultural communication with a vengeance where one of the most frequently recurring problems is matching different musicians' senses of time, which in many cultures are much more fluid and 'laid back', to the demands of rigorous festival and touring schedules. It also put the organisation on another crash course to financial problems.

In 1988 in the midst of this rapid expansion, WOMAD undertook a fundamental reappraisal of its internal administrative structure in a necessary move to more 'professional' management of what was becoming an increasingly complex operation. Such changes, the move to Wiltshire and the growing internationalisation and professionalism meant that what had once seemed an important part of the Bristol alternative scene had up and left causing much local discussion and debate. I suspect this tension between idealism and professionalism is a phenomenon common within new social movements. During this 1987–8 period WOMAD was increasingly being perceived as a white middle-class affair, attracting much local criticism. WOMAD had always had very strong connections with Bristol's black community. Funds were obtained from the Arts Council in recognition of the validity of such critiques and numerous black workers were taken on and continue to play important parts in the organisation. There have been few Asian workers directly employed, though many work within the overall WOMAD support system. Given its ability to enable people to experience festivals and travel all around the world, WOMAD uses its position of power to attract skilled volunteer workers interested in world music and related issues.

The administrative changes split WOMAD into divisions: festival organisation, Real World Records, the WOMAD agency, merchandising, financial/organisational matters, and education. This meant that the organisation had a clear structure and that a double track of hard commercial sense could continue to be combined with often state-funded activities. South West Arts contributed to the setting-up of the agency.

The agency grew from the need to 'tour' musicians. Most of the earlier financial losses arose from the sheer expense of flying in musicians, accommodating and feeding them. If some of these costs could be offset by booking them to other promoters who would also incur the additional expenses, then not only could income be generated but additionally the artists could generate attention, requests from the newly emerging circuit of innovative promoters and established arts organisations could be met and much extra income earned for both the musicians and WOMAD, taking a usual percentage. The key to this operation was for WOMAD to be co-sponsored for many festivals, beginning in 1988, with which the touring schedules could be matched. New workers with agency experience were drafted in during 1989, though from as early as 1987 a new breed of tour managers was being developed.

During the winter months when festival co-promotions were

being worked on simultaneously, artists could be tentatively approached and tours booked. Over the years WOMAD had built up working relationships with specific artists and bands whom they appreciated and whom they found to be reliable. These had to be integrated with new artists in order to introduce variations continually into festival line-ups, as WOMAD has always been committed to introducing unknown artists. In addition individual co-promoters would specify which of the possible artists they wished to engage. It was felt necessary to alter specific rosters in order to attract festival audiences. Part of the agency also was to work with the educational arm of WOMAD so that in the early summer bands could be gently introduced into Britain, instruments acquired, sets built, and acts, where necessary worked at and polished. This was done in conjunction with schools programmes, mainly in the West Country. It involved a network of supportive promoters, schools advisers and arts centres, though in the case of, say, the Cambodian National Dance Company this was achieved in Glasgow in conjunction with OXFAM. In addition, specific artists whom Real World/WOMAD records wished to tour, to tie in with recording, media exposure and record releases, were linked to the agency/festival circuit.

Fine in theory, exciting and innovative as this was, it was the sheer complexity of holding these strands together which led WOMAD into yet another financial crisis in the summer of 1990, precipitating another radical reappraisal and restructuring. It is my view that a recurrent strength of WOMAD has been its restlessness, its willingness to explore new areas and possibilities constantly with the utmost creativity. This has been accompanied by continually working beyond manageable limits, placing those involved under enormous stress, summer after summer. This partially blew up in 1990. The sheer complexity of keeping financial tags on many simultaneous tours, the logistical details of visa acquisition, airfares, accommodation, transport, media exposure, recording radio sessions, film and video segments, generated innumerable small- and large-scale crises. Part of the problem was an unwillingness to delegate enough independence to the various arms of the organisation, the lack of clear enough statements of ends and sheer lack of time to pay attention to the necessary details of day-to-day movement across the world of large numbers of musicians. Any hitch, such as an illness, a missed air flight, a transport breakdown, visa problems, personal crises within bands, could throw this tightly wrought scenario into disarray, generating much unwanted criticism for the organisation as a whole. This in turn would spread throughout the network, altering WOMAD's reputation.

Another result of this style of organisation was dissatisfaction on the part of artists. Whether used to close and attentive treatment if they had previously worked for WOMAD, or just new to the West, they found themselves involved in gruelling tours, punishing miles of motorways with often poor accommodation and food provided for them by local promoters, many of whom were unprofessional and unprepared, if very supportive. Arriving in a strange town, playing to the small hours, driving to many different houses to sleep on floors, night after night was the experience of lesser-known bands. In order to offset costs they would be booked in illogical geographic order – tours need to consider the distances of travel required of artists each day – so that their accommodation expenses could be laid off, thus intensifying pressure on them physically and psychologically. In addition, though weekend gigs would be well paid in Britain, often underwritten by local authorities and arts centres, the other mid-week gigs were often very poor financial propsitions but would be accepted merely to feed and accommodate the artists. Though it was offset by high performance fees abroad and through festival payments, many musicians could not understand why their overall income at the end of the tour, after airfares, accommodation and other expenses as well as agency fees had been deducted, seemed so minimal despite absolutely scrupulous treatment by WOMAD. Finally, many artists could not understand why after a seemingly successful tour, they could not return, not appreciating the pressures WOMAD was under to alter its roster continuously and the exigencies of having to pick certain acts to tie in with record promotion, which meant that others received what they felt to be second-class promotion. The scars of earlier financial crises meant that many of the tours were scrimped: poor transport, too much work and so on led to a feeling of malaise despite the outward-seeming success of the organisation as a whole. WOMAD found itself in problems partly of its own making and partly unavoidable.

The solutions which went into operation exemplify a reflexive and rational response to these pressures. Firstly, the staff was cut by nearly three-quarters. This caused deep anguish and bitterness for many who had worked to the best of their ability for several years and were deeply committed to the organisation. Secondly, much of the agency function was abandoned as too logistically difficult, emphasis being placed on well-known artists who could command good fees worldwide. Smaller or compact well-integrated groups were chosen, cutting costs and problems. Thirdly, the rising number of worldwide co-promotions meant that one festival per week could be held. Linked to these festivals was a deeply thought-out programme of in-depth workshops. This meant that instead of daily touring, artists were moving only once a week, there was a shorter period involved, there was a tight nucleus of artists who would move together worldwide, intensifying the bonds between them and facilitating the musical hybridity WOMAD has always encouraged. The logistical problems of disparate tours could be avoided, and large-scale transport pooled. Block booking of air flights, visa acquisition and so on meant less organisational stress. In many senses the 1990–1 decline of the British boom in world music has not only meant that WOMAD had to 'go international' where the fees are better, thus avoiding having all its eggs in a very depressed Britain; it has also taken the pressure off the complex logistics of day-to-day touring. By holding workshops and festivals weekly, standards of accommodation etc. could be pre-specified and controlled more tightly. A final advantage is that by linking it to workshop programmes the music can be appreciated in much more depth, lessening the superficial 'spectacle' that the previous touring model had intensified. Nevertheless, this workshop strategy has proved difficult to mount within Britain given the constraints on people's incomes during the current recession. Many associated with WOMAD felt in the 1988–90 period that the idealism associated with the educational aspect had been squeezed out by the pressures to tour and go international. One consequence of the new model is that it is other cities, elsewhere in the world, which now benefit at the expense of Britain – except at the British festivals, where support for educational work has deteriorated given the crisis in local government finances and the demands WOMAD itself is under. Doubtless other crises will emerge, new decisions will have to be made, but the heart of WOMAD remains sound.

In 1984, Jameson called for 'a radically new type of internationalism'. WOMAD and the world music movement in general have attempted to play their small part in this journey of exploration. For those involved, time and space may be collapsing but new spaces, new times, continue to emerge even though they themselves may collapse from exhaustion from time to time.

Notes

1 In what follows I use the shorthand term 'world music' to mean a cluster of activities both practical and symbolic, which includes the making and presenting of music, its dissemination through various media and in numerous sites such as gigs, concerts and festivals, and its moments of consumption. There is no such 'thing' as world music per se.

2 WOMAD is an acronym for The World of Music and Dance an organisation formerly based in Bristol, now in Box, Wiltshire, of which more below.

3 I derive the terms spectral and organic from Scott Lash 'Learning from Leipzig', *Theory, Culture and Society*, vol. 7, no. 4 (November 1990), pp. 145–58. The spectral would better be described as aural/spectral. My discussion of new social movements is an attempt to extend the few cursory remarks he sketches vis-à-vis the organic tendency.

4 To cover the full complexity of postmodern theory would take me too far afield.

5 For good overviews see David Harvey *The Condition of Postmodernity* (Oxford, 1989) and Stanley D. Brun and Thomas Lienbach, ed., *Collapsing Space and Time: Geographic Aspects of Communication and Information* (London, 1991). For good empirical material on global news see Roger Wallis and Stanley Baran, *The Known World of Broadcast Media: International News and the Electronic Media* (London, 1991).

6 Here the primary text is Peter Bürger, *Theory of the Avant-Garde* (Manchester, 1984).

7 See Lash, pp. 151–3 and his *The Sociology of Postmodernism* (London, 1990), pp. 172–3.

8 For a statement of his aims see Fredric Jameson, 'Postmodernism, or the Cultural Logic of Capitalism', *New Left Review*, no. 146 (1984), pp. 53–92. For his description of postmodernism being 'more morally horrendous' than all previous moments of modernity see Anders Stephanson, 'Regarding Postmodernism' in Andrew Ross, ed., *Universal Abandon: The Politics of Postmodernism* (Edinburgh, 1988), p. 11.

9 Jameson, p. 88 and pp. 91–2.

10 See Robert Young, *White Mythologies* (Oxford, 1990), pp. 22ff. for detailed rebuttal of foundationalism and its implications.

11 Ernesto Laclau, *New Reflections on the Revolution of Our Time* (London, 1990), p. 10. Full elaboration of Laclau's subtle argument would take me too far afield though as we shall see it is linked to the relational quality of identity.

12 Alberto Melucci, *Nomads of the Present* (London, 1989), p. 232.

13 For a particularly useful and careful account which draws upon Bourdieu's work and emphasises the sedimented quality of much social organisation in particular see John B. Thompson, *Ideology and Modern Culture* (Cambridge, 1990), pp. 146–62.

14 For a subtle discussion of the 'fictive' see Donna Haraway, *Primate Visions: Gender, Race, and Nature in the World of Modern Science* (London, 1991), pp. 1–15 and James Clifford and George E. Marcus, *Writing Culture: The Poetics and Practice of Ethnography* (Berkeley, 1986).

15 Laclau, p. 35 (my emphasis).

16 Melucci, p. 60.

17 Jameson, pp. 61–71. Numerous examples of this kind can also be read in the text.

18 For the best analysis of this condition see Victor Burgin, 'Paranoic Space', *New Formations*, no. 12 (winter 1990), pp. 61–76. He brilliantly teases out the connection between narratives of bodily dismemberment, paranoid space and narcissism.

19 Jameson, p. 92.

20 Anthony Giddens, *Modernity and Self Identity: Self and Society in the Late Modern Age* (Cambridge, 1991), pp. 210–11.

21 Tony Bennett, *Outside Literature* (London, 1991), p. 259.

22 Place and community are no longer necessarily linked. We can simultaneously be 'placed' and belong equally to 'communities' which are dispersed but united by interest, lifestyle and specialisation. See Peter Gould, 'Dynamic Structures of Geographic Space' in Brun and Lienbach, pp. 10–15. Most emancipatory struggles entail just such an attempt to write another history.

23 Laclau, pp. 39–40.

24 For an extremely interesting discussion of these issues as the affect the 'south' and the crucial importance of inherited cultural differences as opening up different paths to different modernities from a Eurocentric one see Thiery G. Verhelst, *No Life Without Roots: Culture and Development* (London, 1990). Vandana Shiva, *Staying Alive* (London, 1990) is absolutely essential on the intersection of the south and gendered difference.

25 Melucci, pp. 89–92. Verhelst argues that these questions of modernity equally affect the 'south'.

26 Lash, *Learning from Leipzig*, pp. 154–6.

27 Giddens, pp. 27–9.

28 Lash, 'Learning from Leipzig', p. 149.

29 Melucci, pp. 109–10.
30 See Richard Middleton, 'In the Groove, or Blowing your Mind? The Pleasure of Musical Repetition' in T. Bennett et al., ed., *Popular Culture and Social Relations* (Milton Keynes, 1986), pp. 170ff., Andrew Chester, 'Second Thoughts on a Rock Aesthetic' in Simon Frith and Andrew Goodwin, ed., *On Record* (London, 1990), pp. 315–25, Phillip Tagg, 'Open Letter: Black Music, Afro-American Music and European Music', *Popular Music* vol. 8, no. 3 (October 1989) and Lash, 'Discourse or Figure? Postmodernism as a Regime of Signification', *The Sociology of Postmodernism* (London, 1990), p. 172.
31 On the complexities of trust see Giddens, pp. 35–69. For the gendered differences in relation to this issue of trust, see Carol Gilligan, *In a Different Voice* (Cambridge, Mass., 1982).
32 Melucci, p. 129. See also on this the paranoid space/body/politics linkage the essential Klaus Theweliet, *Male Fantasies*, 2 volumes (Cambridge, 1989).
33 Melucci, p. 60. For a systematic discussion of the internal structure of such movements and the nature of their segmented, polycentric network structure see Claus Offe, 'New Social Movements: Challenging the Boundaries of Institutional Politics', *Social Research*, vol. 52, no. 4 (winter 1985), pp. 817–68, and Rudiger Schmitt, 'Organisational Interlocks between New Social Movements and Traditional Elites: The Case of the West German Peace Movement', *European Journal of Political Research*, vol. 17 (1989), pp. 583–98.
34 Melucci, p. 136. On hybridity, of essential importance in aesthetic innovation, see George Lipsitz, 'Cruising Around the Historical Bloc: Postmodernism and Popular Music in East Los Angeles', *Cultural Critique*, no. 5 (winter 1986), pp. 157–78, who makes use of the term *bricolage*. See also in relation to visual arts, Hal Foster, 'Wild Signs: The Breakup of the Sign in Seventies Art' in Ross, Universal Abandon, pp. 251–68, and Peter Wollen's brilliant 'Tourism, Language and Art', *New Formations*, no. 12 (winter 1990), pp. 43–60.
35 Giddens, p. 224.
36 I concentrate only on its emergence in Britain.
37 See Andrew Goodwin and Joe Gore, 'World Beat and the Cultural Imperialism Debate', *Socialist Review*, vol. 90, no. 3 (1990), p. 65.
38 *New Musical Express* (24 July 1982), my emphasis. In this section many of the press comments are drawn from WOMAD's own archives and as such appear as comments on previous festivals. I feel that they provide, with a few other sources, a representative selection of the terms available during the period.
39 Mark Kidel, *The Observer* (25 July 1982) and John Hayward, *Record Business* (26 July 1982).
40 Charles de Ledesma, *The Guardian* (20 July 1985).
41 Philip Sweeney, *The Guardian* (22 July 1986), my emphasis.

42 David Amoros, *Folk Roots*, no. 27 (vol. 7, no. 3) (September 1985).

43 Graham Evans, 'Reeling to the Rhythms', *West Africa* (August 1986), p. 16–28.

44 *Music Week* (2 August 1986).

45 See for example *Folk Roots*, no. 43 (January 1987) p. 53.

46 See for example Philip Page, *Folk Roots*, no. 57 (March 1988), pp. 64–5, and Emmanuel Oliver, 'Teaching the World to Sing', *Living Marxism* (June 1989), pp. 38–9 on how introduction of the term redistributed the musical field. See also Ian Anderson's views in *Folk Roots*, no. 98 (August 1991), p. 5, where he writes: 'it was a term that completely underwhelmed virtually all of us who were at the meetings that dreamed it up . . .'.

47 See editorials by Ian Anderson, *Folk Roots*, nos 94, 96 and 98 (April, June and August 1991) for analysis of the state of 'world music'.

48 Chris Stapleton, 'Paris: Africa' in Francis Hanley and Tim May, *Rhythms of the World* (London, 1989), pp. 10–23.

49 Goodwin and Gore, p. 73. Space forces concentration only on this latter aspect and Britain in particular.

50 The texts I have found most interesting are: Emmanuel Oliver; Rick Glanville, 'World Music Mining: The International Trade in New Music' in Hanley and May, pp. 58–67; Paul Oldfield, 'When All the World's a Stooge', *The Guardian* (Friday 1 September 1989); Mark Kidel, 'Vibes Behind the Drumbeat', *The Guardian* (21 October 1989); and Goodwin and Gore.

51 For a useful discussion see Charles Hamm, 'Revisiting Graceland', *Popular Music*, vol. 8, no. 3 (October 1989), pp. 299–304.

52 Rick Glanville, p. 60. This article is one of the best on the really interesting issues of detail concerning world music.

53 Baaba Maal, 'Maal Practice', *Folk Roots*, no. 95 (May 1991), pp. 34–7.

54 Oliver, p. 39.

55 Paul Oldfield, *The Guardian* (21 September 1989).

56 On this facet see Peter Lawrence, 'Do the Rock Papers see World, Folk and Roots Music as One Big Lentilburger?', *Folk Roots*, no. 98 (August 1991), p. 33.

57 Maal, p. 37.

58 Melucci, pp. 60–1.

59 Which term to use here is deeply problematic, for the channels may include subordinate cultures within the West such as Gaelic culture, Sami culture of northern Scandinavia, resistant culture of urban space, women's culture and so on. In this sense I could use 'the other' but let's imagine 'the south' to be a condition immensely variable but similar in its resistance to the centrality of contemporary culture.

60 Verhelst, pp. 72–8.

61 For details see Peter Gabriel interview, *Q Magazine*, no. 32 (May 1989), pp. 70–8, *The Observer Magazine* (20 August 1989) and *The Independent* (Friday 15 July 1988).

62 I point this out to show how there is a sense in which at this early
    stage the types of linkages commonly cited in new social movement
    theory can easily be found.
63 *Now: Toronto's Weekly News and Entertainment Voice*, vol. 7, no. 47
    (4–10 August 1988), pp. 18–19.

Amon Saba Saakana

Culture, concept, aesthetics: the phenomenon of the African musical universe in Western musical culture

African music has been a resilient but partially unacknowledged force in Western popular music for at least four hundred years. Each century, each decade, throws up a new African or African-derived musical influence which perpetuates itself in Western popular music and becomes integrated into the cultural musical style or pattern of Western culture to the extent that its originators are ignored, relegated to a secondary, 'primitive' role and emphasis placed upon the imitators as originators. This essay attempts to place this phenomenon in perspective and to throw some light on the significance, intelligibility and symbolisms of African music which have resulted in misinterpretation, ethnocentrism and disfiguration. Before beginning such an exploration, a note about the term *African*: Euro-American scholars have nominally alienated continental Africans from diasporan Africans in their specific interpretations of musical phenomena. In this essay the word is used genetically: all those who are descended from people born on the African continent, similar to the term *Caucasian* as generally understood in Euro-American scholarship whether belonging to a geographical entity or not.

Clash of modes of production: a context

The historical mode of production in Europe has been based upon slavery, i.e. the mechanism by which wealth was accrued was motored through the existence of classes. This foundation goes back to the beginnings of the first manifestation of 'civilisation' in the Greek city states, with a massive imbalance between free citizens and the masses of the Athenian state, for example, who were slaves. In the African context slavery, as we understand its application from Greece, was non-existent. In the African context a 'slave' could become a leading and influential citizen in the society. There was no legislation to enforce slavery in Africa, although, as demonstrated by Aristotle in *The Athenian Constitution*,[1] slavery was a legal right and any attempt to alter this mode, by Solon in the sixth century BC, for example, led to vilification and attack. Solon had to flee Greece for instituting limited constitutional changes to the condition of the slaves. In Rome this mode of production persisted to the extent that at one stage slaves numbered two to three million,[2] representing 35 to 40 per cent of the population. In Africa, a system of gift exchange, between the king and the state and the general population, did not lead to slavery until the sixteenth century and the arrival of the European.

'System of gift giving provide an important means of distribution of wealth.'[3] The basis of all wealth is land. In Europe land was private property, while in Africa, up to this century and up to now in some places still ruled by chiefdoms, land was entrusted to the monarchy but for use by the majority. No settler could be refused the use of land. Referring to the right of land-allotment of an African prince, Diop says, 'This singular personage . . . , still the master of the soil, in the ritual sense of that term; he is the one who allots land to newcomers . . . He has received the land in trust; he never sells it – he would not dare to do so for religious reasons.'[4] So private property never became a reality until the notorious European laws during the period of colonisation in this century.[5] One is beginning to grasp the fundamental oppositional proclivities of the African and Caucasian modes of production which would involve an aesthetic appreciation or non-appreciation of the cultural models upon which music rests. This could be better understood in the response by Europeans to the culture they were seeing and describing both in Africa and in the Caribbean and the Americas in former centuries, during the period of slavery. Such an insight would give us some historical framework from which we can understand the later responses to African music by critics and non-critics alike.

Clash of cultures: a historical view

In the African context, music-making was an aesthetic attempt to express the sounds in nature. These sounds, from the lion, the

elephant, the bird, the wind, the river, thunder, etc., became the
principle for artistic formulation and expression. Bebey states that
African musicians 'do not attempt to combine sounds pleasing to
the ear. Their aim is simply to express life in all its aspects through
the medium of sound . . . he [incorporates the] natural sounds . . .
into his music.'[6] The position of the jazz musician as an example of
this model can be understood if one compared the 'singing' of a
dove (which I witnessed in Ibadan, Nigeria) in which the dove riff
is repeated endlessly; the jazz musician, as well as other African
musicians globally, organises music from the fundamental concept
of chordal, melodic, or rhythmic repetition. Thus a musically
illiterate Caucasian such as James Phillippo, the eighteenth-century
cleric and landowner, could refer to African musical practices in
Jamaica as 'rude music', 'the most hideous yells from the whole
party by way of chorus . . .', 'discordant sounds', etc.[7] This base
ignorance has been perpetuated in the twentieth-century by no less
respectable a music journal than the *Melody Maker*, which, in 1926,
had an hysterical response not only to a John B. Southar painting,
The Breakdown, of a jazz musician performing before a naked
Caucasian woman, while underneath the musician sits the shattered
body of the Roman goddess Minerva, who supposedly typified
wisdom, but to the *association* of jazz with the African musician.
The lengthy quote which follows is necessary to highlight the
extent to which cultural apprehension expresses an ethnocentric
bias in relation to the perception of race and class of the African
creator. One is not stating, as the dominant Caucasian view
authenticates, that racism is a phenomenon of slavery; rather one is
arguing that the presence of both class and ethnic identity throughout European antiquity, medieval and contemporary times, is an
expression of a particular, more rabid form of racism which the
system of Caucasian economic modes produced. Thus ethnocentrism
and racism are endemic in the Indo-European cradle *before* the
existence of African slavery.

The article was written by the editor who perceived Southar's
work as a threat to the moral fabric of the young, an affront to the
Caucasian female, and a condemnation of jazz musicians, particularly the African creators. The article sets off from a rational point
by praising the painter for his realism and artistic ability, makes
laudatory remarks about the hanging committee of the Royal
Academy (where it was exhibited), and protests that although jazz

musicians are not thin-skinned, the public would inevitably place inferences on the picture that were not there. The writer, however, is obviously warming up to something and it becomes ominously apparent what that something is in the fourth paragraph:

It is not our intention to labour the point, and so to give this picture a publicity disproportionate to its value, but we state emphatically that we protest against, and *repudiate the juxtaposition of an undraped white girl with a black man.* Such a study is straining beyond breaking point the normal clean interferences of allegory. We demand also that the habit of *associating our music with the primitive and barbarous negro derivation* shall cease forthwith, in justice to the obvious fact that we *have outgrown such comparison.*

. . . We see Minerva lying shattered and neglected in the background. It is said that, for the purpose of this picture, she presented the 'old order of things' which the iconoclasm of jazz has hewn down. Minerva, however, was the Roman goddess of wisdom, and the neglect of wisdom . . . is not the indiscretion of our modern dance-loving girlhood . . . but the un-wisdom of the artist himself who so thoughtlessly stressed and unconsciously perpetuated a *phase of human association in its repugnant and least representative form.*

'Breakdown' is not only a picture entirely nude of respect to the chastity and morality of the greater part of the younger generation, but in the degradation it implies to modern white women there is a *perversive danger* to the community, and the best thing that can be done is to have it *burnt.* (emphasis added)[8]

One needs to understand the irrational nature of the article, appealing as it does to the baser nature of the reader, in the context outlined above. In addition, however, to the racial superiority that the writer assumes, one also sees his assumption of Christian morality: that the 'white' woman is of innate moral quality and could only be *debased* by the association with a *repugnant* African jazz musician. The pioneering role of the jazz musician becomes subsidiary to the *cultural prestige* the music has gained as a result of the Caucasian involvement. In other words, the African invented, and the Caucasian imitated and refined. One can make further observations on this notion of 'low-class' cultural origins of jazz: jazz was in fact the creation of the most socially stigmatised African group in the United States. The late ragtime pianist Eubie Blake, born in 1883, wrote of his mother, 'My mother was very religious and hated ragtime like all the high-class Negroes . . . I played it in the houses of ill-repute when I was fifteen.'[9] Yet ragtime was considered as having the 'unselfconscious charm and good manners of late-Victorianism'.[10] At this time, however, ragtime was already appropriated, sanitised and finally regurgitated to the world in an acceptable Caucasian style. This parallels the acceptance of the 'symphonic' Paul Whiteman's demelanised jazz which he popularised in the USA and Britain in the 1920s, for example, and implanted the impression that he represented the refinement from 'the crude jazz of the past'.[11] In line with this model, the *Melody Maker's* editor proceeded to define jazz as 'our music', erecting frontiers between the appropriators and the originators who are still in the *primitive* and *repugnant* phase of, supposedly, *anthropithecus erectus*. This argument expressed all the prejudices and symptoms of the late Victorian world where representations of the 'primitive' society were rampant. Street says, 'The application of evolutionary theory to the ladder meant that researchers could expect to find examples of earlier stages of their own development by examining living contemporary societies.'[12]

Thus the editor exemplified a feature of racism whereby the characteristics of creativity can only have meaning and significance when expressed by the Caucasian. In that he defends both the creativity of the Caucasian jazz musician and the morality of chaste youth. Southar, obviously a politically conscious painter, successfully organised the symbolism of European culture to express the colonial arrangement of British society. The Royal Academy, that bastion of good taste and of mainstream tinkerers, faced with widespread protest (supported by the Musicians' Union) removed the offending picture from public view. One cannot but ponder, however, on the virtue derived from the canonisation and celebration of Roman colonial deities, a society which once colonised Britain and expressed utter contempt for its culture . . . one can understand this phenomenon only in the context of invented genealogies where, through colonial education, the colonised identifies with his coloniser!

One needs to widen the context of understanding, however, if some coherence is to be derived from ethnocentrism/racism as a motor of Euro-American society. The problem of interpretation is encased in the problematic of culture. It is cultural conditioning which is responsible for sensory perception, thus a theoretical comprehension of the necessity of this focus must not escape us. It is the study of music history which should liberate us from our prejudices, one writer proclaims. 'Historical work on popular music requires careful analysis, a detailed knowledge of context, and a degree of sympathy and imagination. The historian is always in danger of making facile generalisations and unwarranted connections. A number of potentially good books on related subjects have been marred by poor historical knowledge and a lack of sociological insight.'[13] Gammond's insight, though valuable, is marred by his lack of detailing the victimising high-class/low-class approach to music by characterising one of Adorno's books as having some 'useful historical and social ideas and observations',[14] rather than interrogating Adorno's racist premises about jazz. Adorno says of Stravinsky's utilisation of jazz ideas, 'Stravinsky experimented with jazz forms precisely in his *infantile* phase . . . Stravinsky reveals, by means of distortion, the *shabby* and *worn-out aspects of dance music* . . . he forces the flaws of this music to speak . . . he eliminates all traits of false individuality and sentimental expression, which *irrevocably belongs to jazz*' (emphasis added).[15] Thus jazz becomes not a model to be influenced and regenerated by, but *shabby* and *worn out*, in addition to being *infantile*. This perception of African music, as has been demonstrated, is confined neither to the explanation of 'during the period of slavery', nor to the 'scarcity' of an African population, but to an innate and automatic reflex system built into Euro-American society which expresses the binary features of class and race bias.

This racist feature is entirely absent in the work of a scholar such as Bruno Nettl who utilises the comparative historical method at all times, thus avoiding the pitfalls which Gammond wrote of so tellingly. He has a firm belief in this method and says,

The study of music requires us to take a certain view of the total repertory from which it comes. A tune such as 'Lord Randall' is really all of its variants, past and present, known and unknown, for the total identity of a piece is also its history. In the case of music in oral tradition, one is usually limited to extrapolating history from recent manifestations, and only in the rarest instances have brave souls tried to reconstruct parent versions from a comparison of the variants recently extant.[16]

This simply means that generalisations about music, especially from a culture different from our own, cannot be made unless serious and methodical scrutiny is made of the corresponding culture from which the music springs. The expression of *perception* of a different musical code usually results in unconscious or conscious comparison with the vocabulary of the music of one's own culture. This becomes particularly distorted in societies, like most of the Caucasian Western world, in which untrammelled destruction was expressed on the other's culture, resulting in both colonialism and the denial of the features of civilisation (after, as Lévi-Strauss says, they had been destroyed!).

This brings us back to the invented genealogies of historical and contemporary European societies in claiming Greco-Roman civilisation as the foundation stone of European culture. As Bourdieu points out, the notion of cultural influence and absorption is usually 'integrated into the pantheon of the Greek or Roman as a particularly successful achievement of "human nature" in its universality'.[17] He confirms that this process of appropriation appears to be the 'sole right of the middle class' and that it emerges as 'the relics of an aristocratic past'.[18] In today's world, however, appropriation is not confined to the middle class, and continuously asserts itself in all segments of British popular life where the mainstream, in our view, still dominates, and thus sets the tone for the behaviour and conformity (in spite of so-called radical appearances) of those contributing to the imagined pantheon of innovation. A brief examination of the African and Euro-American world view, in so far as perception or cognitive interpretation of culture can serve as a reminder of a penetrative and comparative cultural holistic vision, is a necessary precondition for the critic or historian of music.

Aesthetics or ways of seeing

The simplest form of cultural differences are noticed in the range and type of clothes worn by Africans and Euro-Americans. Before the late 1960s, a road sweeper in England would wear a tie to clean the streets. In the Caribbean the people who did this job were dressed as everyday people. If one did not know that the Englishman was a road sweeper, one would logically assume that he was an office worker. Clothes, therefore, are the simplest indicator of cultural style. Africans, no matter where they are born, have a penchant for brightly coloured clothes, for bright ornamentation – gold, for example, can be worn on all fingers, or one's teeth (as in the Caribbean and the Americas) can be fully goldcapped. In Europe this is viewed not only as ostentatious but as gaudy and exhibitive. The problem with this vision is that, because of the rabid class system, modes of dress defined one's class position. This can be taken to the level of language: in the Caribbean the greeting of a long lost friend can commence with curses – 'Yuh bitch! Where yuh was all this time!' Sometimes, this could be taken to a more extreme degree where the persons could actually swear at each other, talking in loud voices, then fall into each other's arms! Aesthetically, this is showing one's appreciation for one's friend on the most emotional level. The exuberance of these codes can produce a corresponding response of horror in the Euro-American. He/she may even go so far as to call the police! Africans' parties, even today in Britain particularly among young people, can be loud and run from midnight until the following evening. This frequently results in British neighbours informing the police and the subsequent banning of these parties.

Encoding emphasis on the bass in African music can be contrasted with pop musical styles before the advent of reggae, in which treble was far more significant. In rock or heavy metal, mixed-down music focuses on 'top' or treble sounds. Even in European classical music violins, treble, dominate the sound. In African-derived music the bass is mixed with the heaviest emphasis to express rhythm and emotionality rather than cerebrality.

What we are outlining is that what is the aesthetic canon in one society may well be the opposite in another. In the context of dance, ballet is based upon unnatural dance postures – pointing, and rigorous physical exercises which enforce the necessity of artificial physical development, and constant diet to maintain slimness and small breasts.[19] At ballet and European classical music performances, the audience is not expected to participate in the experience, but applaud politely at certain high points or preferably at the end of the performance. If one contrasts the dance posture and training of the African dancer, one inevitably ends up with an entirely different expectation. Amongst the Akan, for example, there is the belief that 'good dancers must not hold themselves "as erect as the stalk of a plaintain"'.[20] The opposite is true in ballet. Does the European classical musician anticipate the involvement of the audience? Except in applauding, this is certainly not the case. In Africa, the Caribbean, and in the Americas, this is certainly not true of musicians. 'The presence and participation of an audience influence the animation of a performance, the spontaneous selection of music, the range and textual improvisation, and other details; and this stimulus to creative activity is welcomed, and even sought, by the performers.'[21] The opposite is true in European classical music: the conductor, a single person, selects the range of the repertoire, controls the playing of the performers, and the flow of the music with a baton. Such an unnatural performance of music would be inconceivable to an African.

The training of the musician is also perceptually different. In the African context, music is learnt through the physical relationship of the teacher to the pupil, and through oral presentation. In Europe (at least over the last two hundred years), the opposite holds true: the musician is taught from notation and printed texts. Thus the models for the two cradles can be seen to be operating from differently inherited musical canons, in teaching and in performance: 'The child who will grow up to become a player on the talking drum is helped by the master drummer who taps the rhythms on his shoulder blade for him to get the sensation of the motor-feeling involved. When he has to learn musical rhythms, he is taught appropriate sentences or nonsense syllables which convey the same sort of rhythm.'[22] In terms of the transmission of musical knowledge, Charlie Mingus, the late jazz composer, said that he had played the instrumental parts of his compositions to the different musicians: 'I decided to memorise the compositions and then phrase them on the piano part by part to the musicians. I wanted them to learn the music so it would be in their ears, rather than on paper, so they'd play the compositional parts with as much spontaneity and soul as they'd play a solo.'[23] At a rehearsal in New York, one witnessed the response of bassist David Williams to an upbraiding by the band leader that he was playing out of rhythm when the former responded, 'I was looking at your feet'! This implied that he was accessing the pace of the composition by the rhythm tapped out by the leader's feet. That we have the establishment of different musical or aesthetic canons should be obvious. The following piece of information conveys the most startling contrast to the Euro-American emphasis on the marks of civilization: 'Since antiquity, Yoruba have adorned their cheeks with lines. *They associate line with civilization.* "This country has become civilized" literally means in Yoruba "This earth has lines upon its face." Civilization in Yoruba is *ilàjú* – face with lined marks' (emphasis added).[24] In the Euro-American context, civilisation has a plethora of associations embodying forms of dress, language, literacy, buildings, financial status, concepts of mythology and history, etc.[25] These contrasting examples of aesthetic considerations in the African and Euro-American world view exemplify the dilemma of the music critic or historian in his or her response to a musical culture seemingly disorganised and arbitrary. What we have tried to outline is the contrasting aesthetic paradigms or canons that go into animating the inner organism of musical cultures without which a proper appreciation of musical style or form would be inevitably lost. A cursory glance at the history of popular music unveils the mask of appropriations which have been paraded as the genuine article, or as in the name of the African-American inventor, the real *McCoy*.

The African origin of Western popular music

The process of naming is a fundamental aspect of African philosophy and religiosity. The Dogon's concept of *Nommo*, the word, is fundamental to an understanding of the development of the universe. Similarly, naming in Kemit (ancient Egypt) was precisely the process which initiated the advent of the present world. Atoum-Ra says, 'I the evolver of the evolutions evolved myself . . . which came forth from my mouth.'[26] It is this concept which runs through the spectrum of Black African thought and it is this disposition which brings us into conceptualising the meaning of African music in its own terms, and in contrast to Western popular music. Symbolism is widely understood to have particular meaning within the context of African art, and in relation to music it expresses itself in the *processes* and *procedures which structurally define African music*. 'Symbolism', writes Mveng, 'has as its mission the *transformation* of the world into a *language* . . . Rhythmical art subordinates this transformation to rational laws and *recreates the world according to the will of Negro-African genius*' (emphasis added).[27] Kwabena Nketia, in defining the broad areas of continuity of the structural paradigm of African music in the Americas and the Caribbean, says, 'it appears that the *primary value* of what exists in Africa is that it provides a *basis* for the development of tradition, for exploring new directions without *loss of musical identity* . . . That is why African roots must be viewed in terms of creative processes which allow for *continuity and change*' (emphasis added).[28]

We are thus developing an understanding of the complex basis which informs the context within which New World African music develops: by naming what this music is we understand its special language of symbolism, thus communication, and its avowed predilection in transformation of the given qualities of its traditions, as well as its new encounters, and the resulting processes which develop from this. That is to say, in recreating a language of communication, the music as we now understand it, renews itself from its traditions incubated in Africa. The identifying ancestor is undeniably Africa: basin of cultural paradigm and features of connective atavism.

This final phase of our argument is to demonstrate that, in spite of new encounters and the obvious influence which result from this, the thrust to maintain an African identifying base has prevented African New World music from becoming, as is the norm, part of the cultural melting pot, of absorption and loss of identity. By briefly surveying the historical implantation of African music, in spite of new instrumentation – which one maintains is merely a *technical* development of tradition – within Euro-American music, one can derive some idea of its generative and renewing function in contact with different cultures.

Military music
Farmer shows that by 1753 the instruments which characterise military bands in Britain and the rest of Western Europe were composed of wind instruments. This, he argued, was based on the influence of Germany, on a genre he referred to as 'the old *Harmonie Musik*' which consisted of 'two oboes, two clarinets, two horns and two bassoons, which was not unlike the arrangement of the Royal Artillery Band at its formation in 1762'.[29] What is quite apparent is the absence of percussion instruments. Farmer believes that this was primarily due to the attitude of the German band masters and that of the officers 'who would consider drumming as quite alien to their conception of the time honoured *Harmonie Musik*.'[30] Beyond the prejudice against percussion instruments, Farmer cites the actual military code which prohibited specific forms of instrumentation: 'The use of Drums, or Trumpets . . . to be avoided as much as possible.' But the next prohibition (1788) shows that some form of percussion was already in use for it makes

definitive reference to it as an agent which varies '*the times of march, they create noise, prevent that equal step which habit alone can give the troops, and tend to destroy the very end they mean to promote.*'[31]

These prohibitions were soon to change with the introduction of *Janitscharen Musik*, which originated in Turkey and became popular in Eastern, then Western Europe: Russia, Poland, Prussia (Germany), then Britain. According to Farmer, this popularity came via stage musicals which featured lively Turkish musicians and dancers: the instruments used were bass drum, kettledrum, cymbals, triangle, from which developed a number of small bells whose appellation was 'jingling Johnnie' and was later superseded by the glockenspiel. 'Originally, genuine Turkish performers were engaged to play these instruments, but as these died or were discharged, negroes took their place.'[32]

The introduction of African musicianship completely changed the status of military music in Britain. 'The effect on the general public was *astounding*. For the *handful* of onlookers which had hitherto been attracted by the marching army band, *crowds now thronged to see the latest craze . . . the forbiddance* of the 'Band,' as the Horse Guards had laid it down, *became a dead letter . . . No other music necessitates so solid, determinate and striking a beat. It is almost impossible to get out of step.*' (The last italics are Farmer's, the others this writer's.) Farmer goes on to show that the necessity of tempo as a strict time-keeper was enforced on the army, drum-majors being ordered not to deviate in the most minute way from the number of steps taken by the band member in relation to the function of the percussionist. 'With such aids we may be sure that *tempi* were regulated to perfection in the Royal Artillery by the "Blacks".'[33]

What is being suggested is obvious: that the introduction of percussion instruments into the British military definitively altered its music. Though this introduction was first carried out by Turkish musicians, it was only when African musicians projected a new style of playing, from the African model, that true popularity and appreciation of this music became a reality. The extent to which this popularity could be judged, as Farmer shows, is the extent to which rival military bands utilised a fantastic number of percussionists – sometimes one-third of the band – to the imbalance of the music.

Orchestral manuoeuvres in the dark

It can be extrapolated, hypothetically, that this innovation would have had some effect upon British and European music in general, and we can point specifically, as Farmer shows, to the incorporation of new rhythmic ideas into European classical music. 'It is true that the cymbals and bass drum had been used once or twice earlier, but it was not until Mozart in *Seraglio* (1781) and Haydn in the *Military Symphony* (1794) employed these implements for the "colorisation of rhythm", as Berlioz said, that these alien instruments came to stay. Today they take their place quite naturally in orchestral scores.'[34] The range of African-derived influences in European classical music is wide and only passing mention can be made to it: as Mozart and Haydn responded to the musical demands of their times by incorporating new rhythmic conceptions into their music, so too had ragtime played a seminal role in compositional ideas for the innovator Debussy in his *Golliwog's Cakewalk* (1905), which, according to Eileen Southern, 'bounces along in typical ragtime song with a syncopated melody in the right hand and "um-pah" accompaniment on the left.'[35] Southern goes on to show the extent of ragtime's influence on modern European composers at the turn of the century: 'Stravinsky wrote *Piano Rag-Music* (1920), *Ragtime* for eleven instruments (1918), and included a ragtime movement in the popular *L'Histoire du soldat* (The Soldier's Tale, 1918). The French composer Erik Satie (1866–1925) wrote a ballet, *Parade* (1917), in which the *American Girl's Dance* is in ragtime style . . . All of this music reflects the captivating but rather vapid style of the ragtime song rather than the essence of serious rag music.'[36] A note needs to be added to this last from the master himself, Stravinsky, 'I felt so weak after my long bout with influenza that I found it impossible at the moment to undertake anything at all fatiguing, and therefore occupied myself with work that I *imagined would not overtax my strength* . . . As the work progressed, I saw that my task was by no means so *simple* as I had imagined, and it took me *six months to complete it*' (emphasis added).[37] The work in question? *Ragtime*.

We need, however, to state that genuine innovation has always been mediated by perverse (commercial, financial) considerations: that the oscillating definition of 'commercial' has accumulated a meaning which veers from the traditional. Commercial music, during the eighteenth century, merely meant popular, i.e., the composer was living professionally off his earnings, and there was popular response by the public to hear this new music. However, with the incipient centre-staging of African-derived music, and the concomitant invention of traditions (which has been a constant in most societies, now grasping a new identity owing to a change in fortune of their circumstances), there has been a distancing of *new* popular musics being accepted as 'serious' for a variety of reasons. One of these reasons is the status quo, the identification, in later times, of the middle class with *classical* music, and the same identification maintained by the post-imperial/colonial European world in their responses to Africans and their musical creativity. Thus serious music = good, and popular music = vulgar = jazz or African-derived music.[38]

The plantation/ministrelsy model

Although the United States is regarded as the incubator for the popularity of African-derived songs, it was in Britain that returning adventurers brought what they thought they heard back to notate, publish and perform. Britain had already popularised these African-derived songs as early as the mid eighteenth century, and it was with Mungo Park that one of them became popular. He had 'taken' the song down in Africa (the inaccuracy of notation was notorious amongst Europeans) and sent it to the Duchess of Devonshire who promptly indigenised the song by altering its lyrics to conform to the popular rhyme, as well as interfering with the natural phrasing of the song. In addition, she sent the song, *The Negro's Humanity* or *A Negro Song*, to a composer friend, Giacomo Ferrari, who continued the 'doctoring'. Not only did it become famous, but several other composers created their own versions of it.[39] This trend finally gave way to the gross interpretation of African life on the plantation which led to stereotyped figures such as Zip Coon, the city slicker, and Jim Crow, the field hand. These figures became a passionate commercial pastime for Americans and they initiated the advent of *blacking up*, the act of imitating the song, dance and mannerisms of the African, whether city or country based. These satirical and caustic images pandered to the racist proclivities of the Euro-American and opened a tremendous taste for this type of performance. Many Euro-American careers were made this way.

'For more than four decades', writes Southern, 'Ethiopian

ministrelsy was the most popular form of theatrical entertainment in the United States and, *to the rest of the world, America's unique contribution to the stage'* (emphasis added).[40] The source of these songs, of course, continued to be the African. They were actually modelled on authentic songs or melodies and recast in the mould of Euro-American cultural style, that style seriously modified in its contact with the African. Thus the reflection was a dilution. This, however, ignited the advent of another awareness: the African himself became a performer in his own imprisoned image, but with the possibility of displaying an authentic, uniquely thrilling cultural style. One of the most famous of these African American per-formers was William Henry Lane, popularly known as Master Juba, who has been canonised in African American folklore. According to Southern, novelist Charles Dickens, on seeing him perform, remarked that he was 'the greatest dancer known'.[41] These performers, both Euro- and African American, inevitably implanted and sustained an image of stereotype of the African which conformed to popular notions of behaviour: happy-go-lucky, indolent, criminally inclined, etc. But the fact that the popularity of the style and form of the music transcended its racial origin is reflected in the national folk repertoire of the United States.

The jazz craze and development in Britain
One can only briefly sketch in the available information and some added details about the history of jazz in Britain. George Melly, that popular fixture in British popular culture, openly stated on a television programme that 'black' music and culture were a magnet for people of his generation, that he felt he could sing, speak and affect the mannerisms of the African American singer. In an instructive series of articles during the 1970s, Harry Francis, former musician and journalist, wrote, 'In Britain we had little knowledge of jazz history. True, some of us had heard of the Original Dixieland Jazz Band and others at work during the few years following the first world war, but we had then tended to think of it as a *new development in popular music'* (emphasis added).[42] Francis was not incorrect to think of jazz as a trend in popular music, but the fact that he used the verb *tended to* implied that it was other, perhaps more esoteric, more exotic, thus able to fulfil a personal predilection, as Melly had confessed. What is significant about the growth of jazz in Britain, however, is the fact that

once the original, African American, sources had been located and listened to, the likes of Paul Whiteman could only hold a middle of the road interest. We are speaking here of the differentiation between the quality and value of the original innovators as cultural indicators as against their marketability.

This last remark is important in order to designate the position of the African creator, who is acknowledged as the source of invention and innovation, but was confined to a limited circuit and ambiance, without the concomitant financial rewards reaped by his lesser copyists. In this context, for example, one can compare the very early success of Spike Hughes who, grounded in the exposure to the Caucasian imitator, 'soon switched his allegiance to the work of Ellington and Fletcher Henderson'.[43] Francis described Hughes's relationship to the development of British jazz as a 'milestone', and says that 'We were not therefore surprised when, in the Spring of 1933, Hughes went to New York to organise three recording sessions *with a Negro orchestra*, that there were to be found among its personnel *many of those who had worked with Henderson*' (emphasis added).[44] One can not only see the importance of the African American model, but link into the connections between present Euro-American trends in locating the purveyors of current musical styles in order to capture the spirit and the feeling but expressed in the vocal style of the Euro-American: Paul Simon with reggae, samba and South African musical styles; David Bowie who set a trend in the middle 1970s by recording with the Philly sound of Gamble and Huff; Peter Gabriel and his African flirtation; Vanilla Ice with his African American rap musicians and dancers; Sting in his former role as lead singer of the Police, a reggae act, and his later excursions with jazz players; Lisa Stansfield, whose voice is indistinguishable from the African American performer's; and George Michael, the Greco-British sex model of House music. These are only a few of the links with the innovator-imitator model whose history in music stretches back to the mid eighteenth century.

The other important feature that one ought to note in the development of British jazz is the role of the Caucasian musician as sideman in the book of the African American musical stars. Francis records one such incident when Louis Armstrong toured Britain in 1932: 'he was, in fact, persuaded by his advisors (ill-advisors would perhaps be a better description) to replace the West Indians by a

band of British white stars . . . The result was *disastrous*. . . . [45] On
his return in 1933, Armstrong formed a band, according to Francis,
with the assistance of multi-instrumentalist Leslie Thompson,
African Caribbean, comprising mainly African Caribbeans. In a
conversation with the deceased clarinettist, Rudolph Dunbar proclaimed to this writer that he was in fact the person who had
arranged Armstrong's band. Regardless of the arranger, the band,
according to Francis, was 'excellent'.

It is obvious that African Caribbean musicians played a seminal,
but hardly acknowledged, role in the formative years in British
jazz development. Just how much can be read by the following
scenario. The Southern Syncopated Orchestra, led by Marion
Cook, famous African American musician/composer, toured Britain
in 1919 and played before King George V at Buckingham Palace.
When some members of the band (some thirty-six pieces) died in a
boat which sank on the way to Dublin, the orchestra reorganised in
1921 and included several African Caribbeans, among whom were
Cyril and George 'Happy' Blake and the distinguished organist
Wendell Bruce-James. The British bandleader Ted Heath, who
also played with the band, wrote of 'the assistance given by
members of the group to the British contingent on aspects of jazz
playing.' Bruce-James, who was by no means a jazzer, nor was the
band acknowledged to be, strictly speaking (although it performed
jazz numbers), wrote a series of articles on the Kinema organ for
the *Melody Maker* in 1928. He was followed in 1931 by Rudolph
Dunbar who wrote a similar series for the *Melody Maker* on how to
play the clarinet. Dunbar subsequently printed a course book on
the clarinet and opened a school for clarinet playing in the middle
1930s. Students came from as far away as northern Europe and
Germany; the book went through thirteen impressions until as late
as 1961. Dunbar was followed in 1933 by Reginald Foresythe,
bandleader, composer and arranger, who also wrote a series on
the piano. The extent to which African musicianship pushed the
threshold of musicianship in Britain to a higher level, both on the
theoretical and on the practical levels, cannot be done justice in
this essay; we can only point to some of the highlights and the
personalities.[46]

Ken 'Snakehips' Johnson, in terms of swing, was regarded as a
pioneer in British jazz history: the fact that he was not a musician
but a dancer and bandleader tells us something of his charismatic

personality. A band started and fronted by saxophonist Leslie Thompson had won a contract for a night club through Johnson. Thompson, who was the first to front an African jazz band in Britain, auditioned and was employed. It seems that the band, being successful, had its contract renewed, but by Johnson. Two of Thompson's band members subsequently left and joined up with Johnson.[47] It was from this incident that Johnson's name became synonymous with jazz – his brilliant dancing and showmanship greatly helping the band's reputation as one of the best in Britain. However, Johnson died tragically in 1941 on the stage of the Café de Paris in London. An eulogy in the *Melody Maker* referred to him as 'THE KING IS DEAD – LONG LIVE THE KING!'[48]

African musicians also showed up significantly in popularity polls. In 1944 Carl Barriteau's band was voted the no. 3 dance band and he ran no. 2 as the favourite soloist, while in the clarinet section he was no. 1; Joe Deniz was no. 2 guitarist, while Leslie 'Jiver' Hutchinson was no. 1 on the trumpet, and Yorke de Souza was no. 2 on piano. In 1949 Ray Ellington (no relation to the Duke, and not African American) was voted the no. 1 in the small band category, while Coolridge Goode (who still in 1992 plays at the age of 75) was voted the no. 2 bassist. In 1960 Joe Harriott beat Johnny Dankworth to the position of best alto-saxophonist. Dankworth had admitted in a 1957 interview that there were other (African) musicians better than he and named trumpeter Dizzy Reece and Joe Harriott.[49] In 1962 Cleo Laine, Shirley Bassey and Elaine Delmar (the daughter of Jiver Hutchinson) were voted no. 1, 2, and 4 as best female vocalist, Joe Harriott again no. 1 and Harold McNair no. 5, Shake Keene, formerly *the* star at the London University band, was no. 1 on the flugelhorn, while Frankie Holder was no. 1 on the bongos. All these popularity polls appeared in the *Melody Maker*.

Conclusion

One can only summarise the important contributions African musicians – from the United States, the Caribbean, Europe and Africa – have made to the development of popular music in Britain. In the case of military music the records clearly demonstrate the specific areas in which African musicians innovated. Although this essay has confined itself only to the percussion element, there were concrete contributions in the area of brass and reed instruments. In jazz, one can clearly see the impact of African American recorded music on the consciousness of the Caucasian musican. That the Caucasian musician privileged the playing and arranging abilities of the African American in employing them to enhance their work and reputation at home is historically validated. Individual musicians also stand out, as does the pioneering work of Joe Hariott who was acknowledged by the Modern Jazz Quartet as having the ability to give a hard time to America's best. It should be added that the *Melody Maker* consistently reported on new African Caribbean musicians as they entered Britain: it was anticipated that they would inject a new standard of musicality into British dance music (jazz). They also appeared at the annual music jamborees and were reported to have performed well. The other element is that of racism, which created a tremendous hazard for African musicians in England from the level of management. Many jazz musicians, as well as African musicians' managers, frequently reported that racism was experienced by African musicians. They were confined to playing the club circuit in London, prestigious as they were, but toured limitedly in the provinces. Such bands as Jiver Hutchinson's and Reginald Foresythe's were reported to have broken up as a result of racism.

In the area of Latin music, Edmundo Ross is widely acknowledged as the pioneer. Whether his music was pioneering is not the question, but his popularising of it is undoubted. Calypso (kaiso) also made a tremendous impact in Britain in the 1950s and influenced some of the trends in popular music. In relation to the era of pop music and money-making – the 1960s – the work is too enormous to go into here, but it is sufficient to state that musicians like John Myall, John McLaughlin, Georgie Fame, and many others, received their inspiration not only from African popular music but from African musicians who, because of the racist orientation of the popular press and the music industry itself, never made it to 'stardom'. Reggae, soul, funk, rap, House, and West African music, have definitively shaped the contours and path of Western popular music. It has been confirmed, through the words of the pop artists themselves – from Mick Jagger and John Lennon to the latest crop – that they were all shaped and defined by African popular music.

The significance of these trends cannot be lost upon us, nor can the changing fortunes of the African musician/performer in the Western world be put down to the modification of racism – one must clearly understand these trends from the formidable role that African-owned record companies (Trojan in London, Gamble & Huff, Stax and Motown in America before their sell-out or conspiratorial collapse) played in the fortunes of the multinationals, CBS, Warner Bros., Polygram, etc. The presence, therefore, of the African in the recording industry has added an important competitive edge psychologically and financially, which has forced the multinationals to deal with the success and popularity of new musical trends. In 1926, for example, as Jones[50] points out, the category referred to as *race* records, was confined to anonymity until the giant corporations saw the selling power of this music and intervened to expand their own profits.

The African musical universe continues to inject and infuse new areas of innovation into Western popular music to warrant the fundamental question: is Western popular music really Western? A thorough examination of this question inevitably leads the scientific researcher to the conclusion that the African musical universe, beginning with Kemit (ancient Egypt) which haunted and influenced Greek philosophers, has always been a part of the phenomenon and canon of what we consider to be Western popular music.

Notes

1 Aristotle, *The Athenian Constitution* (Harmondsworth, 1984), p. 43.
2 Quoted in Alan Watson, *Roman Slave Law* (Baltimore and London, 1987), p. 2.
3 Alan P. Merriam, 'The Bala Musician', in Warren L. d'Azevedo, ed., *The Traditional Artist in African Societies* (Bloomington and London, 1975), p. 251.
4 Cheikh Anta Diop, *Precolonial Black Africa* (New York, 1987), pp. 149–50.
5 See A. T. Nzula, I. I. Potekhin, A. Z. Zusmanovich, *Forced Labour in Colonial Africa* (London).
6 Francis Bebey, *African Music: A People's Art* (London, 1975), p. 3.
7 James M. Phillippo, *Jamaica: Its Past and Present* (London, reprinted 1969, pp. 242–3).
8 *Melody Maker*, vol. 1., no. 6 (June 1926), p. 1.
9 See Foreword by Eubie Blake to Peter Gammond, *Scott Joplin & the Ragtime Era* (London, 1975), p. 7.
10 Gammond, p. 11.

11 Quoted in LeRoi Jones, *Blues People* (London, 1965), p. 100.
12 Brian Street, 'Reading the Novels of Empire: Race and Ideology in Imperial fiction at the Turn of the Century' in David Dabydeen, ed., *The Black Presence in English* Literature (Manchester, 1985). p. 97.
13 Vic Gammon, 'Problems of Method in the Historical Study of Popular Music' in David Horn and Philip Tagg, ed., *Popular Music Perspectives, Papers from the First International Conference on Popular Music Research*, Amsterdam, June 1981, published by the International Association for the Study of Popular Music (Göteborg and Exeter, 1981), p. 29.
14 Ibid., p. 28.
15 T. Adorno, *The Philosophy of Moden Music* (London, 1973), p. 171, ff.25.
16 Bruno Nettl, *The Study of Ethnomusicology, Twenty-nine Issues and Concepts* (London, 1983), p. 110.
17 Pierre Bourdieu, 'Outline of a Sociological Theory of Art Perception', International Social Science Journal, vol. XX, no. 4 (1968), p. 590, note 3.
18 Ibid., p. 612.
19 For an excellent discussion of this and the problems of anorexia and constant physical injury, see Lucy Cavendish, 'Stars in their Eyes, Pain in their Art', *The Guardian* (19 July 1991), p. 19.
20 H. Kwabena Nketia, *The Music of Africa* (London, 1975), p. 33.
21 Ibid.
22 Kwabena Nketia, 'The Musician in Akan Society' in d'Azevedo, p. 89.
23 Charles Mingus (as told to Diane Dorr-Dorynek), liner notes to *Blues & Roots* Atlantic, ATL 50232, 1960, reissued 1976.
24 Robert Farris Thompson, 'Yoruba Artistic Criticism' in d'Azevedo, p. 35.
25 For a deeper discussion of this see Amon Saba Saakana, first chapter in *Colonialism & the Destruction of the Mind: Psychosocial Studies in Class, Religion and Male/Female Sexuality in the Novels of Roy Heath* (London, 1993).
26 E. A. Wallis Budge, *The Egyptian Book of the Dead* (New York, 1967), p. xcix.
27 Engelbert Mveng, 'The Function and Significance of Negro Art in the Life of the Peoples of Black Africa' in *1st World Festival of Negro Arts, Colloquium on Negro Art* (Paris, 1968), p. 15.
28 Kwabena Nketia, 'African Roots of Music in the Americas – An African View', *Jamaica Journal*, no. 43 (n.d.), p. 17.
29 H. G. Farmer, *History of the Royal Artillery Band: 1762–1953* (London, 1954), pp. 51–2.
30 Ibid., p. 52.
31 Quoted by Farmer, ibid. and emphasis by the author from David Dundas, *Principles of Military Movements* (1788), p. 53.
32 Ibid. The reference to the glockenspiel is contained in Farmer, *Memoirs of the Royal Artillery Band* (London, 1904), p. 51, note 1.

33 Ibid., p. 102.
34 H. G. Farmer, *Military Music* (London, 1950), p. 37.
35 Eileen Southern, *The Music of Black Americans, A History* (New York, 1983), p. 329.
36 Ibid.
37 Igor Stravinsky, *An Autobiography* (London, 1975), pp. 78–9.
38 For a discussion of these ideas, couched in the language of jazz/ classical music, see Henry Pleasants, *Death of Music? The Decline of the European Tradition and the Rise of Jazz* (London, 1961), particularly pp. 129–30.
39 Southern, p. 89.
40 Ibid., p. 91.
41 Ibid., p. 95.
42 Harry Francis, 'As I Heard It . . . Jazz Development in Britain 1924– 1974, Part One', *Crescendo International* (March 1974), p. 4. This and a large part on jazz history in Britain was researched by Ricky Smith on a project we started jointly in 1984. I owe a great deal to Ricky's painstaking research and for far more information which is barely summarised here. The results of this joint research may be published later in book form.
43 Ibid., Part 6 (August 1974), p. 8.
44 Ibid.
45 Ibid., Part 8 (October 1974). The other references in this paragraph are culled from this article.
46 For further information, see *Melody Maker*: Bruce-James, September 1928, p. 1034; Dunbar, November 1931, p. 917; Foresythe, 3 June 1933, p. 17.
47 Leslie Thompson and Jeffrey Green, *An Autobiography* (London, 1985), pp. 92–3.
48 Leon Cassel-Gerard, 'Who is There to Take Ken Johnson's Place?' *Melody Maker* (22 March 1941), p. 5.
49 *Melody Maker* (3 May 1958), p. 7.
50 Jones, op. cit., pp. 100–1.

Alexander Laski

The politics of dancing – gay disco music and postmodernism

What is postmodernism?

Postmodernism as it stands today is a highly complex and often seemingly contradictory theoretical framework. Through its development it has not only grown progressively more complicated in itself, gradually extending its range of application, it has also engulfed other theories such as post-structuralism, which, being at root a theory of language, has given a philosophical slant to much postmodern theory. This essay will begin by drawing out some of the most salient elements of a postmodern theoretical framework and giving a brief description of the meanings of certain key terms and concepts. After this general introductory exposition, there will be a discussion of certain phenomena in gay disco music for which postmodernism seems to provide a good analytical framework. Following this, problems of applying postmodernism to gay disco music will be discussed. Finally, conclusions will be drawn regarding the possible validity and use of postmodernism in analyzing cultural artefacts, and in this case particularly gay disco music.

Despite its seemingly complex and contradictory nature, postmodernism can ultimately be reduced to two major concepts: the free play of signifiers and the end of metanarratives.

The free play of signifiers means that signs no longer have any connection to their referents. Signs refer only to other signs, meaning can only be understood on the surface level of sign interchange which creates a web of intertextual superficial meaning. Because of the signs' lack of basis in a referent, there cannot be said to be any fixed meanings in signs. The meanings can and do constantly change, they are in a constant state of flux. Any meanings that do happen to be attributed to a sign are arbitrary and short-lived, and there is no recourse to deep meaning, to essential values, to an underlying conceptual structure. At its most extreme, there is no specific meaning to any particular word. A word can mean anything, or a word can mean nothing.

A metanarrative is a structure, or pillar of conceptualisation. Metanarratives have been (and continue to be) used by academics and theoreticians to divide the world into blocks whose meaning is more or less visible and fixed. There are metanarratives of history, of race, of sexuality, of logic, of truth and so on. Postmodern theory claims that such clear-cut divisions no longer exist, or at least are in the process of being broken down, their boundaries being eroded. Class, for example, as presented in a Marxist analysis is seen as no longer applicable, because the classes as described by Marx no longer exist. Some postmodern theory would claim that the metanarratives as traditionally understood have never existed, that they have always been the result of ideological manipulation. The end of metanarratives is closely linked to the free play of signifiers. Without fixed meanings, the static structure of a meta-narrative simply cannot exist.

The above description is very general, and is in fact a deliberately reductive overview to demonstrate the fundamental principles of postmodernism. Within the free play of signifiers and the end of metanarratives, there are many more subtle concepts proposed to explain the social and cultural situation we find ourselves in at present. These too can be linked together into certain categories whose meanings seem to be relevant to each other, although it must be borne in mind that all of these refer to the two major principles already discussed. The categories which seem to need some elucidation in this context are: electronic technology, authenticity and authorship; intertextuality, retro mode and pastiche; style and image over content and meaning; fact and fiction, fantasy and reality, hyper-real and euphoric experience. This is not all that is ever meant by the word postmodernism, but is that which seems most directly relevant to the subject of this paper.

The rapid rise of electronic technology throughout this century, and particularly since the Second World War, has caused major problems in theories of art and culture.[1] The huge expansion of mass-produced works of art has had several results. The first result is that there is a globalisation of artistic media in that world markets are flooded with the products from other countries. Also, countries which are economically and politically weak end up with a diet of products from the richer and more powerful countries. International barriers are crossed and there is an ever-increasing cultural colonisation by countries such as the USA in particular. The second result of mass distribution of products is that the original is lost, if indeed it can be said that there ever was one. It is not like reproductions of the *Mona Lisa*, which if necessary can be referred back to the original in the settlement of artistic or academic disputes. What can be said to be the single original copy of an episode of *Dallas*? Mass production (and consumption) is also fast-moving and fast-changing. It is by its nature highly complex, requiring large amounts of money and many people to produce each work.

The searches for either authenticity or authorship in a work of art are both spurious searches in postmodern theory: authenticity requires fixed, deep and essential meanings, meanings which have their roots in metanarratives. For example, authenticity is often seen in terms of human interest, in what it means to be human, and works which are authentic are those in which the true values of being human are dealt with in a realistic yet sympathetic way. In postmodernism, the quality of humanness is in itself a metanarrative which relies heavily on other metanarratives, such as that of history and that of truth. In view of postmodern claims regarding the end of metanarratives, the authenticity of human values is greatly destabilised. Authorship too is the search for an essentially human source, this time for a single recognisable individual. Not only does this rely upon a belief in essential human values, it also needs a metanarrative of the individual, or the subject, for it to be relevant. The 'death of the subject' (Jameson, p. 63) is the postmodern claim that the individuated psychological subject that is generally taken for granted does not exist – in fact, that it never really did exist, and this subjective identity (the 'bourgeois individual' (Sampson, p. 3) or 'sovereign subject' (Hebdige 1989, p. 51) was created and maintained ideologically by social groups who had a great deal invested in such a subjective identity. Without the belief in the unitary, self-reliant individual, the subject is 'decentred' (Lash and Urry, p. 288). There is no longer a core identity, an underlying belief in one's individuality. Self-image is formed from constantly shifting interaction with other surface images, with no possibility of anchoring it to any essential or fixed identity.

The concept of intertextuality, extremely important in postmodern theories of art and culture, includes the so-called 'retro mode', pastiche and parody. Intertextuality is the situation in which works of art refer to other works of art in the same or a related genre, in fact, in which signs refer to other signs in the same or a similar genre. For example, television programmes referring to other television programmes, films referring to other films and so on. The meaning of such a sign is not allowed to escape from the confines of its genre, it is not allowed to develop. Although the meaning of a sign may be very different in its referred use, it has not really moved forward. If anything it has moved backwards or even across, but certainly not forwards. Such references undermine the belief in development and progress which were so central to modernism.

Retro mode (or 'la mode retro' (Jameson, p. 66)) is a very clear referencing of the past. It can be seen as a ransacking of images, fashions and other signs from the past. It can range from one or two subtle references in a work of art to a pastiche of the entire style of an artist or a period. The claim that postmodernism incorporates both the end of history and simultaneously a use of historical material seems contradictory, but it must be remembered that the past being referred to in the retro mode is not intended to be read as real. It is in fact an extremely nostalgic view of the past, of a re-invented past, of a past that never really existed at all except in the present-day imagination. Thus the retro mode combines the end of the metanarrative of history with an anti-progress view of art which is also intertextual.

Style and image over content and meaning relate quite directly to the postmodern free play of signifiers. To read an artefact (or a performer) by style or image is to read its superficially available information. Postmodern theory claims that products are produced with a heavy emphasis on style, and that they are consumed in relation to their image and not to their use (Baudrillard, p. 206; Lash and Urry, p. 288). Styles and fashions are quick to change and seem arbitrary. The specific manifestations of a fashion (for example the size of a shirt collar) have no deep meaning. They do not refer to any inherent value in a short or a long collar. It is true that particular social groups use specific fashions as badges of group identity, but even this can be arbitrary, and its meanings can be forever evolving and changing.[2] The distribution of image and style is intimately linked to the electronic media, particularly television, and, as such, all the results of the global expansion of mass-produced electronic art forms also apply to the extension of the power and influence of certain (culturally based) fashions and styles. The fashions coming out of the richest and most powerful countries come to be defined as the norm, as having almost a neutral cultural reference, and other more localised fashions are termed ethnic. The barriers of class, race, nationality, even sex are broken down by the constant bombardment of images from a dominant culture, images which even within that culture are arbitrary and ever-changing.

Fact and fiction, fantasy and reality, life as a hyper-real or euphoric experience – these are all extremely important concepts in postmodern theory. Postmodernists claim that we can no longer distinguish between fact and fiction, between fantasy and reality, and that the result of this inability is to experience life as hyper-real and euphoric (Jameson, p. 73; Lash and Urry, p. 287; Hebdige 1989, p. 51). In postmodernism, words and concepts have no fixed, intrinsic meanings and in effect a word can mean absolutely anything or absolutely nothing. For this to be so, the whole concept of truth is no longer a valid one, and the division between truth and falsehood no longer exists. This is the end of the metanarrative of truth. If there is no longer any identifiable difference between truth and falsehood it is no longer possible or even desirable to try and differentiate between them. Fact and fiction are no longer opposites. They are not even the end points on a sliding scale. They simply do not exist.

Postmodern theory claims that much if not all of our experience is learnt via the media, particularly via television (and it must be remembered that television is not a single form, but a fusion of many different artistic and cultural forms). The media is full of fantasy. Even the news has to be entertaining, and as such is highly selective about what it shows, being famously prone to exaggeration for a good story. Soap operas, situation comedies, films, the news, documentaries all seem to be dealing with the same range of signs and are thus all transmitting interchangeably similar messages. The distinction between reality and fiction in the media is so eroded that it ends up being non-existent. People watching come to mistrust the truth of the news as well as believing in the fantasy of the fictional forms. This situation is further exacerbated by the fact that media forms such as film, soap opera, even news, are short and very limited and as such they have to reduce often large and complex issues into neatly-packaged, small and simplistic forms. The stories and even more importantly the emotions become extremely concentrated. The fact that people are said to learn so much of their behaviour patterns from such forms means that they attempt to live their lives at the same concentrated level. They live a great deal of their emotions through the film or soap opera itself, and they try to carry such concentrated emotional experience out into their everyday lives as well. This creates an experience of life at a hyper-real, euphoric level, with perceptions heightened and distorted to the point where everything becomes a fantasy. There is no more reality to counterpose against this fantasy, and as such the concept of fantasy also disappears. Meaning is transmitted from one surface sign to another indefinitely, never referring to deep meaning, never having recourse to an essential truth, to a historically and socially understood system of human values. As with all areas of postmodernism, the signifier has no meaning beyond its inter- actions with all the other free-floating signifiers.

Postmodernism and its use in analysing gay disco music

Before looking at the specifics of gay disco music, some definition of the genre must be made. Gay disco music, as a discrete analys- able unit, is rather difficult to pin down. However, there are certain types of disco music which are aimed at the gay market and which are particularly popular, and as such these are particularly relevant for this essay. These types come under the generic heading of High Energy (usually shortened to Hi-Energy or Hi-NRG) and they include Boystown, Italobeat, Balearic beat, Eurobeat among others. In this essay I shall be using the generic term Hi-NRG to describe, albeit rather simplistically, all these various forms.

Gay disco music, for the purposes of this chapter, I am defining as those records which have appeared in the gay disco charts, taken from the gay press, which are compiled from records played in the major discothèques (usually in London) such as Heaven, Bang, Copacabana and so on. This does not *necessarily* mean that these records are bought in the same proportion by the disco-goers. The use of such charts is of course a simplification of the concept of gay disco music, in that much of the music is also popular in non-gay discos. However, for analysis and discussion purposes, a boundary has to be drawn, and in this case it is the disco charts in the gay press which form such a boundary. The very fact that there exist gay disco charts which are differentiated from non-gay disco charts strongly suggests that there is a range of dance music which gay people feel has specific importance to them. Whether this music is unique to the gay discos, or whether it is mainstream music which is interpreted and used in different ways by gay disco-goers is not really relevant. What is relevant is the existence of the gay disco charts, and this is why I am using these as the basis of my discussion.

One area of production that is common in gay disco music is the re-issuing, remixing, remaking and (re)discovery of records, groups and singers. There are two principal ways that this is done. The first is the referencing of other stars and records (both in terms of remakes of songs and also less obviously by making reference to other stars etc. who have a relevance to the people who might make use of gay disco music). The second is the re-issue of records by groups who have not been popular for some time, and the espousal of their fashions etc.

The referencing of other stars and the remaking of older gay disco records is very common and can clearly be seen by perusing the gay disco charts. A selection of examples will be discussed here which seem particularly interesting, in that they refer to bands who frequently remake older records, or they are records which have been remade many times, or they refer to other stars (and even artistic forms) in rather oblique and subtle ways.

'Cha Cha Heels' (1988) by Bronski Beat and sung by Eartha Kitt has a complicated set of cultural messages from at least three sources. Firstly, Bronski Beat is known as a gay group. It is the first generally-popular openly-gay group. Although by the time of 'Cha cha heels' its line-up was in fact different from its original line-up, it still carries importance as a gay group. Secondly, although Eartha Kitt is somewhat older than the usual singer of Hi-NRG music, she does nevertheless fulfil many of the other required criteria – she is female, glamorous and black. During the 1980s she has also been fairly successful as a singer of gay-orientated disco records such as 'Where is my Man?' (1983) and 'I Love Men' (1984), so by having her singing on their record, Bronski Beat is referring to her other records as well as to their own previous history. In addition to this there is an even more subtle reference in the record. The title of the song refers to a scene in John Waters's cult film *Female Trouble* (1973) starring the late Divine in which Divine (playing a delinquent sixteen-year-old school girl) wrecks her family Christmas and storms out of the house wearing a green baby-doll nightie because her parents did not buy her the requested cha cha heel shoes as a present. This is not only a reference to John Waters's film(s), which have always been popular with gay audiences (John Waters is numbered among gay film-makers and the films are full of drag, homosexual references and characters and so on), but also a direct reference to Divine. Divine was popular as a cult figure both as an actor, and also, importantly here, as a singer of Hi-NRG music himself (with records such as 'Shoot your Shot' (1982) and 'You Think You're a Man' (1984)). 'Cha Cha Heels' was released shortly after Divine's death in 1988, and is a tribute to him. A disco record seems a fitting requiem.

The original Bronski Beat split up, one part retaining the same name and producing the aforementioned 'Cha cha heels' among other records which are not relevant to the discussion here, and the other part, in the form of Jimmy Somerville, going on to form a new group with Richard Coles, called the Communards. The Communards have produced much original music, but they have also had success with remakes of gay disco records. 'Don't Leave Me this Way' (1986) and 'I Feel Love' (1984) are both relevant here. 'Don't Leave Me this Way', which was a general as well as a gay disco success, has been released by several other groups, and has been successful as such each time round in the gay disco charts (it was released by 'Slip' in 1983 and by Jeanie Tracey in 1985; it was also several times in the charts in the late 1970s). Each version is very much a replication of the one that preceded it, in other words, they are not differentiated remixes. Following this, the Communards released a new version of 'I Feel Love' in 1984, which was originally a hit for Donna Summer in 1978 and which was also remixed by Patrick Cowley (who was the producer of many of Sylvester's records among others) and released again in 1982. The Communards' version also includes Marc Almond singing. As with 'Cha Cha Heels', there are several references here.

The first is the obvious reference to Donna Summer, who was one of the original disco divas (and continues to be popular still, almost fifteen years after her first hits and after having undergone three quite distinct periods of production.[3] Donna Summer made herself somewhat unpopular with the gay world by saying publicly that AIDS was the vengeance of God and was just desserts for gay men for living such a dissolute lifestyle. The Communards' version of 'I Feel Love' is a claiming of the song while discarding the singer. The inclusion of Marc Almond is a secondary reference in this version. Marc Almond's records such as 'Tainted Love' (1981) and 'Memorabilia' (1981) have been very popular in gay discos, and Marc Almond himself has been considered to be a gay (or at least non-straight) singer. Thus this record refers to the gayness of the Communards, the importance of Donna Summer as a gay disco diva and her place in the history of gay disco music, as well as to Marc Almond and all that he implies.

After the split-up of the Communards, Jimmy Somerville has continued his career as a solo singer. He has recently issued a remake of 'You Make Me Feel (Mighty Real)' (1990). This was originally a hit for Sylvester in 1979. Sylvester (who died in January 1989 at the age of 41), is, like Donna Summer, one of the original superstars of gay disco music. The remaking of one of his most popular songs is a homage to him. It is interesting to note that after the success of Jimmy Somerville's remake, Sylvester's version itself was re-issued in a remixed form (1990). The Jimmy Somerville version refers to the Sylvester version, and the remix of the Sylvester version refers to both Jimmy Somerville's version and to his own. Bronski Beat, the Communards and Jimmy Somerville's versions of popular gay disco records refer not only to the stars in question, but also to the past, to a pre-AIDS golden age of disco when the whole experience was new, exciting and unfettered by the gloom of the AIDS cloud. That this golden age never existed as imagined is not really relevant. Despite AIDS (or because of it), homosexuality is more open and visible than ever before, yet the harking back to the imagined good old days is very strong in remakes of records by the great stars.

The song 'Maybe This Time', originally from the musical *Cabaret*, and made famous by Liza Minelli in the film of the same name, was released as a disco record in 1983 by Norma Lewis. This refers out of the disco genre but not out of things considered important to the people who make use of gay disco records. Liza Minelli's status is that of one of the great stars, partly because of her appearance in such films as *Cabaret* and also because of being the daughter of Judy Garland who is considered one of the most popular stars ever in a gay sensibility.[4] The film *Cabaret* (based on the novel *Goodbye to Berlin* by Christopher Isherwood) has long been popular with gay men because of its relatively sympathetic and open portrayal of homosexuality. The release of a disco version of 'Maybe This Time' alludes to Liza Minelli, to *Cabaret*, to Christopher Isherwood, and even to Judy Garland and to decadent early 1930s Berlin. It incorporates all of these into the gay present, the world of the gay disco. It involves different cultural and artistic genres as well as causing temporal confusion in that it is a 1980s disco record referring to a 1970s film referring to a 1930s past. These seem telescoped into one time, that of the present.

Liza Minelli has herself recently been in the gay disco charts with 'Losing my Mind' (1989) and 'Love Pains' (1990). It is not the first time that 'Love Pains' has been in the gay disco chart. It was originally sung by Yvonne Elliman in 1982 and then by Hazel Dean (one of the most successful Hi-NGR stars) in 1988. Both of Liza Minelli's recent successes were produced by the Pet Shop Boys, who have also been successful in the gay disco charts. The Pet Shop Boys (who are considered a gay group) not only 'rediscovered' Liza Minelli, they also made a record with Dusty Springfield, 'What Have I Done to Deserve This?' (1987). They have thus taken stars from the past who have not recently been in the public eye and re-popularised them. This is an important part of the gay disco's tendency to re-issue records by groups who have not been popular for some time, and to re-discover singers from the past.

The re-discovery of bands in their own right is also evident in gay disco music. An obvious example is the resurgence of popularity of Abba in the mid to late 1980s, but there have also been re-releases of records by Boney M (an album of their greatest hits in 1988), Sylvester ('You Make me Feel'), Baccara ('Yes Sir, I can Boogie' in 1989), Petula Clark (with an updated disco version of 'Downtown', called 'Downtown 88' in 1988), and there have been records in the gay disco charts by Debbie Harry ('In Love with Love' in 1987), Olivia Newton-John ('The Rumour' in 1988), Barry Manilow ('In Search of Love' and 'I'm your Man' both in 1986) and even Raquel Welch ('This Girl's Back in Town' in 1987). All of these refer back to earlier times of gay disco itself, to pre-disco days, and also to stars and musical forms that do not seem directly disco-orientated but which are felt as having relevance for the disco-goers.

All the re-issuing, remixing, remaking and (re)discovery of

records, groups and singers invoke several of the tenets of post-modernism. The first is the fact of signs referring to other signs and not to anything else, and the second is the nostalgia, the looking to the past and not to the future. All the examples mentioned above deal in signs, signs in gay disco and also signs in other genres which are considered to be related in some way. It could be said that they all relate to gay experience, but in themselves, they are no more than signs referencing other signs. The success of 'Maybe this Time', for example, relies on it referring to the signs of other forms, which in turn reinforce the signs in the newest version. The specific signs which are seen as important can and do alter and can seem rather arbitrary. It is only their relationship with other signs that prevents this apparent arbitrariness from sinking to the level of meaninglessness. Each important sign exists at the meeting point of a network of other signs, which in turn are also interstices of other signs and so on. This lack of deep meaning in the signs, along with their disregard for linear development (in that they refer back or across but not forward) causes a temporal and historical confusion. This confusion in its turn causes uncertainty in the future and can lead to an even greater investment in (supposed) past values. The overall viewpoint is extremely nostalgic, it looks backwards, or at best is static. It certainly does not progress. Nostalgia is a safe and cosy retreat from contemplation of the future, or even of the present.

The next important group of postmodern concepts which can be applied to gay disco music is that of electronic technology, author-ship and authenticity. All records released today are in effect elec-tronic products, and are dependent on such technology for their creation, distribution and consumption. This is true even of records of classical music, in that without the highly developed electronic technology, classical music could still only be enjoyed live. With much modern pop music, and particularly dance music, the rela-tionship is even stronger, in that many of the sounds themselves in the records are electronically produced. Electronic production is extremely complex, involving large numbers of people throughout the entire process ranging from singers, musicians, song writers, studio engineers and so on. In such a complicated production, it is virtually impossible to pinpoint the original creative source. It is simply lost in the process. Thus no single author can be named. A postmodern analysis would certainly agree with this, but it would also go a step further. A postmodern view of authorship is that is not only does not exist now, but that it never did. The concept of a single creative source (in other words a specific individual) implies a faith in the core identity, or unitary subjectivity of individuals. As already described, in postmodern terms this is a false belief. Without such faith in the unitary subject there can be no author of a work.

The re-makes, re-issues and remixes of many disco records undermine further the concept of authorship. Not only do mass-produced works not really have an original in the same way that a painting does, the existence of further versions invalidates any claims to originality of the first version. It is not possible for example to claim that the Sylvester version of 'You Make me Feel' is more original or valid than the Jimmy Somerville version. Each has its own validity and worth both in relation to and also separate from each other. The first version may be unknown to someone who enjoys the second version, or the second version (the so-called cover version) may be considered to be a much better version. Equally, who is the author of the Jimmy Somerville version? Sylvester or Jimmy Somerville? Both of them? The person who wrote the song in the first place? It is not possible to state who the author is owing to the nature of production of the records and owing to the confusion of originality.

Two other areas of disco record production which cause problems for authorship are the extensive use of sampled sounds and also the creation of 'on-the-spot' records by club DJs (scratching or other techniques) using bits and pieces of other records. Scratch records (and other records using similar techniques) are dance records produced in clubs by DJs. They are made by interweaving short exerpts of selected records with other sounds (including a pre-recorded bass line) and sometimes to the accompaniment of talking or singing over the top by the DJ. The record excerpts are often so short or so mixed up with other sounds that they are not recognisable, and even if they are, each one only forms a small part of the new track. Any idea of an author of such a track is impossible. Even the DJ is not really the author in that he has made a collage of other people's work, and as such is not an author in the way the word is generally understood.

Sampling involves the electronic reproduction of a pre-recorded sound in which the sound, which can be a voice, a car engine or anything else, is recorded and is then simulated by a computer. It is no longer the original sound in that it is simulated, yet it sounds just like it did in its non-simulated form. This causes legal problems[5] as well as problems of authorship and authenticity. The sampled sounds that we hear are simulated sounds and are thus not considered to be authentic, yet we hear them as authentic, and we react to them as if they are authentic.[6] We are left feeling slightly cheated but at the same time wondering whether it really matters if the sounds are authentic or not. Not only this, but the situation becomes such that it is no longer possible to define authentic (or real) sound, because we do *really* hear and experience the sound, so how can it be said to be inauthentic or unreal?

At this point it is clear that the search for a single author, and also the desire to know if our music is authentic or not, amounts to a desire for a fixed, identifiable and human source to our music. An authentic record is one which has a human source, with what it means to be human and all that this implies. From a postmodern viewpoint, there are two basic problems with this. The first is that the technological nature of record production takes it away from any human source it may have had. It is so channelled, altered and manipulated via electronic media that it almost becomes a machine creation. This is particularly so for modern disco records. The second problem of human authenticity in postmodernism is the very concept of humanity, the metanarrative of humanity. To talk of authenticity in terms of human values is an essentialist position, implying deep and inherent human qualities in every person. These assumptions that are made in referring to such qualities are relied upon in any discussion of real or authentic human values in any work of art. It is considered that human authenticity is what gives one work of art greater validity than another. In postmodern terms, such a reliance on accepted common-sense attitudes regarding the nature of being human are wrong. There can be no inherent (or innate) values of humanness. All meaning is culturally relative. It is also arbitrary, and therefore there can be no such thing as inherent meaning at all. The metanarrative of humanness has been eroded to the point where it is redundant, or it has never in fact existed in the way that we believe. Either way, it is not possible in any postmodern framework to claim such values as authorship or authenticity of a work.

Mass distribution of electronically produced cultural artefacts (whose distribution is also dependent on the same technology) produces an endless supply of fast changing forms. The speed of change destabilises any possibility of meanings becoming fixed in the messages expressed by the artefacts. No sooner does a pattern of meaning seem to be gaining some hold than another message (sign) barges in and replaces it. This happens globally, irrespective of national or cultural boundaries, creating a whole generation of people in all corners of the world who consume very similar cultural messages. In the view of some postmodern theorists, this creates a mass population of undifferentiated subjects who have in this way lost their unique core identity. This weakened core identity in the consumer is further exacerbated by the fact that it is also impossible to pinpoint the identity of the creators of the cultural artefacts that are being consumed. The rapid rise and spread of electronic technology is a vital factor in the development of such a situation.

Style and image over content and meaning is another of the tenets of postmodernism which seems to offer much for an analysis of gay disco music. Generally in pop music, the style and image of the group (and particularly the lead singer) is considered vital to the success of any records that the group produces. It could almost be said that the style of the singer is in effect the meaning of the record. There seems to be a strong correlation between the type of music (in this case mainly Hi-NRG) and the type of singer, in that most Hi-NRG singers are youngish, glamorous black women. The styles and images of other performers of gay disco music are also important. There is the extravagance of performers such as Divine and Sylvester, the boy-next-door (but nevertheless gay) images of Jimmy Somerville and Andy Bell of Erasure and so on. It is claimed that we consume images rather than products, or at least that we consume *through* the image and not through the meaning of a product. This seems to be consistent with a postmodern approach, but it is at this point in the analysis that problems begin to occur.

The problems of postmodernism in analysing gay disco music

If records sell via style and image, and any meaning they are thought to have is arbitrary, then why do some records sell and others not? Many groups seem to fulfil the necessary criteria, have large financial backing and plenty of media exposure, yet they fail to be successes.[7] Is it really possible that people buy a record for no apparent reason, on a whim, and with no thought to what that record means for them? The meaning of any particular record may have different connotations for different people, but this does not disallow it meaning.[8]

Certain social groups identify strongly with particular types of music or group or singer. In the world of gay disco, the most immediately apparent type of singer is female and glamorous, preferably black and fairly young (Donna Summer, Diana Ross, Miquel Brown, Sinitta, Grace Jones and so on to give just a few of the most famous examples). Precisely why glamorous black women should be so popular seems to be a very complicated issue, and outside the scope of this chapter. However, whatever the reasons for the adulation of this type of singer, there is clearly some form of identification being brought into play. Without such identification, there could be no such thing as gay disco music. For a social group to identify with a particular type of music and singer over a period of time would suggest that such music and performers have definite meanings for the social group. It may seem strange that the singers of gay disco music are generally so unlike the people who go to the gay discos, and that this situation is quite unlike that of other subcultural music-based styles (whose fashions tend to reflect those of the relevant singers and bands), yet this fact in itself is conveying important messages about the nature of being (subculturally) gay and how this differs from being, for example, (subculturally) black in Britain.[9]

The patterns of types of music and performer that can be seen in gay disco music imply that there is a real meaning for gay men in such music and performers. The readings that are made of the records are not necessarily apparent either to people who do not listen to such music or indeed to the people who do, yet the readings are there. The readings are in effect meanings and without reasons underlying such readings they would probably not exist and would certainly not have any meaning. It is sometimes believed that people are duped (or more euphemistically, persuaded) to buy records, but, as mentioned, this does not explain why some groups succeed and some fail despite similar hyping. Again, meaning for the consumer is perceived to exist in particular groups and singers, meaning which is considered lacking in others. This is a clear choice between the meaning perceived in one cultural form over the lack of meaning in another. There is a binary division being made between valid and invalid, or authentic or inauthentic music. These sorts of choices cannot easily be dismissed as pure ideological manipulation, nor can they be said to represent confusion of perception on the part of the consumer. Such claims are high-handed (positioning other people and defining their lives for them) and are also inadequate to explain the choices made between what seem, on the surface at least, to be interchangeable musical and stylistic forms.

All the examples of gay disco records given earlier were very specific. They were referring to particular songs, singers or groups. The framework in which they were viewed could in fact refer to any pop music, and not just gay disco. Examples from almost any area of pop music could be given of intertextuality, retro mode, remaking and re-issuing of records and so on. The concepts can be applied to gay disco music, but disco music is not a unique example of such ideas. Pop music generally draws heavily on past music and fashions and even on fashions and symbols from other cultures (Culture Club's use of the star of David and Boy George's espousal of traditional Japanese clothing, among others). During the 1980s there have been revivals of fashions and music from practically every decade of the twentieth century and at present there is a strong psychedelia revival (which developed out of the House music from 1988 onwards). So gay disco music's nostagia is part of a wider retro mode that occurs throughout the pop industry.

The ways in which gay disco music have been seen in a post-modern light could also be applied to other non-musical genres such as video, film and a whole range of television genres like comedy, documentary, quizzes and so on. The various politicians who appeared in the (video) advert for the album *Bananarama the Greatest Hits Collection* (1988) were in effect free-floating signifiers. The Comic Strip's fictionalised programme about a rock band, *More Bad News*, which included real rock singers' opinions of the fictional band, is a conflation of fact and fiction in that it becomes unclear just who is or is not a real rock band. This was further demonstrated by the fact that the fictional rock band in the television programme had some success in the national charts, being thus given the status of a real rock band. Films which reference other films are common, as are rather complex references within films themselves, such as in *His Girl Friday* where the actor Ralph Bellamy is described as looking like the actor Ralph Bellamy (Bordwell, Staiger and Thompson, p. 2). Television documentaries about the making of a film or another television series are also popular. One of the best examples of an intertextual form is the television quiz about television such as *Telly Addicts*. Presumably the quiz could ask questions about itself while it is still being broadcast.

For the patterns of postmodern theory to be clear and valid, it seems necessary to apply them across a wide range of cultural forms. In other words, it is not appropriate or relevant to try to apply them to any very specific area of analysis. This renders it difficult if not impossible to try to claim that they have validity for such a focused area as gay disco music, in that the claims made for postmodernism in the light of gay disco music could be as easily made for any almost any area of modern music production. As such, postmodernism's usefulness in analysing a small specific area is questionable. In the deliberate creation of cultural artefacts, as an aesthetic of production rather than an analysis of the same process, postmodern theories do however still have some validity. This is in fact the way that the term was first used.[10] As a creative aesthetic, postmodernism is very limited, and it is interesting to bear in mind just how much its meaning has been expanded from its original use. If it is true that postmodernism as an analytical theory is valid only if applied generally rather than specifically, then this easily leads to a situation in which trying to apply it becomes so complicated that it is almost impossible. Given postmodernism's disavowal of the concepts of truth and reality, and its claims that life is experienced in an ever more complex and confusing way, then this complexity of application might well seem deliberate. A deliberate vagueness and lack of clarity in postmodern theory seems to be consistent with its lack of belief in truth, yet if this is so then it also seems to be rather contradictory or even self-negating.

This self-negation is in fact a fundamental problem in postmodernism. For postmodernism to be taken seriously, then its own framework must be able to be applied to itself, and yet if this is done, then it, just like everything else, no longer has any claim to being true or correct. Without a concept of truth versus falsehood, there is no appeal for any cultural artefact, academic theory, etc. to deep or inherent meaning in an underlying value system. Such a value system is said not to exist. In this light, postmodernism can be dismissed along with everything else as being nothing more than one theory among many, with no more inherent validity (or truth or meaning) than any other, and possibly less. Yet for postmodernism to be accepted as a general theory of culture, as *the* theory of the culture of our time (in that we are said to be living in a postmodern age), then it must claim to be correct, to be true and this must imply that all other theories are basically on the wrong track. How can a theory which refuses to accept the concept of truth convince us that it is correct? How can it even begin to try to persuade us that it has the answers that other theories do not provide? This is simply not possible. If postmodernism as a theory manages to convince us that it is indeed correct, then it has denied its own position. If it remains consistent, then it cannot make claims to being more true or correct than any other theory, and it, just like everything else, has no ultimate recourse to meaning or truth (Itkonen).

It seems therefore that there are great problems for postmodernism in claiming itself to be the cultural theory of our time. This makes postmodern analysis of social and cultural patterns not only complex but ultimately self-negating. It is also difficult to apply postmodernism as a theory to very specific areas of cultural forms in that its tenets are too general for this purpose. It is thus left to see whether there is value in using postmodernism as a creative aesthetic in the production of cultural artefacts. As has been mentioned, this was the original use of the term and it seems to offer real possibilities. There is however a fundamental problem here as well. If the creative process of an artefact (be it a building, a novel, a record, etc.) is carried out with a deliberate postmodern emphasis, then clearly there has been intention on the part of the creators. Intention, or intended meaning, cannot really exist in postmodern theory in that it implies a primary reading of the artefact which is the same in practice as a deep meaning. Thus creative intention is also problematic for postmodernism. The expansion in the applicability of the term postmodernism (which was never intended in its original use) causes problems even for this limited original coining of the term. From an original intended use which in itself was identifiable, relatively fixed and not denying any meaning in the works created, postmodernism has expanded so far as to mean that absolutely everything is uncertain. There is no deep meaning, no roots, no eternal truths or values that can be called upon as ultimate arbiters of meaning. Everything is floating on the surface, loosely interconnecting with everything else.

If postmodernism had remained a limited creative aesthetic then it probably would not have finished up with the fundamental problem of self-negation. If postmodernism is to continue to be useful, it will have to find a way out of the cul-de-sac that it has backed itself into. If it does not, then it will most likely be discarded. The only other option, that of accepting it with its self-negation, renders all analysis, all research, all thought even, redundant because everything is denied.

Conclusions

It appears that the above description of the self-negation in postmodern theory would make it useless in every way, but this is not necessarily the case. In terms of making sense of the cultural forms that we have defined as gay disco music, postmodern theory might not be able to provide answers, but it can help in seeing the relationship between gay disco music and other cultural forms in that what applies to one can also be applied to many of the others. Using postmodern concepts to see the way in which gay disco records are produced also seems to have some validity (at least as an aesthetic of cultural production). However, for these uses to be available, the most extreme conclusions of postmodernism, its denial of truth and meaning and thus of intentionality and so on, must be ignored or at least put aside.

Postmodern theorists have correctly pointed out certain patterns that do seem to be occurring in our society at the present time. These include an increase of intertextuality, retro mode and pastiching in our works of art, the blurring of the boundaries between fact and fiction in media like the television, the ever-increasing desire for people to live a faster life of heightened perceptions (taken from the cultural forms around them) and so on. These are relatively straightforward and demonstrable. It is with its more extreme claims that the useful foundations of postmodern theory begins to be shaky. The death of the subject for example is highly problematic in that it does not acknowledge a person's right to self-definition, it simply tells a person that his/her definition of him/herself is wrong. This is not good enough. Also, all the postmodern (and post-structuralist) theorists carry on publishing as differentiated individuals under their own names, claiming both the financial and social rewards of their work (and the correctness of their position), while espousing a theory which denies this very possibility.[11] Postmodern theorists do not like having their work confused with the work of others, and yet if there is no unitary subject and no individual authorship, how can this possibly matter? This is merely one example among many of the problems for postmodernism.

To re-emphasise the most important point, the real problem for thorough and all-encompassing postmodern theory is its denial of logic, truth and reality. There is no point in postmodernists claiming this, because in the act of claiming it, they are denying it. The only sensible solution, if one wants to carry on making use of some of the more applicable observations of postmodern theory, is to discard the extremities and restrict oneself to a very limited framework – in effect, that of cultural aesthetic rather than social theory. Whether this can be done, or whether it will prove itself to be useful enough to bother with must remain to be seen. If postmodern theory adamantly maintains that it must be used in its totality as a theory of society for it to be consistent and make sense, then it seems likely that it will not survive and that it will be replaced by less contradictory and more internally consistent theories.

Notes

I would like to thank Richard Johnson and Bernard Devlin for their many invaluable comments and suggestions during the preparation of this chapter.

1 Walter Benjamin (1977) discusses in this essay, among other things, the problem of originality and creativity with regard to mass-produced and consumed works of art. He is referring particularly to film, but much of what he says could be applied to popular music. Briefly, mass production is said to obscure the original (and thus also the creator) in a mass-produced form in a way that painting, for example, does not (although mass-produced copies of the *Mona Lisa* for example can lead to a similar effect). This essay is an early introduction to postmodern ideas of creativity, originality and authorship, and the problems of mass (electronic and mechanical) reproduction.

2 Hebdige (1979, p. 93) mentions the fact that what was originally the subcultural style of the Jamaican rude boys was picked up and appro-

priated by British skinheads. Initially this skinhead image had no
racist connotations, but it has since come to acquire them. Thus what
was once a distinctly black style has become a very anti-black style.

3   Donna Summer's early period was under the production of Giorgio
Moroder; this was followed, after a gap of some years, by a period
being produced by Quincy Jones. Her most recent period, still going
on, is under the extremely successful British production team of
Stock, Aitken and Waterman.

4   The importance of film stars in the gay sensibility is only touched
upon in this chapter, but it needs to be stressed. The old Hollywood
glamorous stars are still much admired in gay culture (stars such as
Mae West, Garbo, Dietrich, Monroe, etc.). This admiration (which
can reach the level of idolisation) has in more modern times been to
some extent transferred on to pop stars, such as Madonna. Modern
pop stars have in some ways replaced the old film stars in social
meaning. Modern film stars do not generally receive the same adulation
as the older film stars or the modern pop stars. (Bronski 1984, Dyer
1982, Hayes 1981).

5   Black Box's 1989 hit, 'Ride on Time' (which was incidentally Britain's
best-selling hit of the year as well as being voted best record in most of
the consumer surveys carried out in the gay press) used the sampled
voice of the American singer Loletta Holloway. Eventually, the producers of 'Ride on Time' paid Loletta's record company, Salsoul
Records, an out-of-court sum. The actual legal situation is nevertheless very unclear (information from *Smash Hits* (21 March – 3 April
1990), p. 10).

6   Goodwin (1990, p. 266) claims here that it is misguided to conceive of
electronically produced music in terms of real or authentic versus
unreal or inauthentic sound. He says that a simulated handclap might
as well be a real one in that it '*really* produces certain physiological
effects when you dance to it'.

7   Rimmer (1985, pp. 144–5) argues that simply hyping a band does not
guarantee its success. He mentions various bands who were greatly
(and expensively) hyped, who looked as if they had the makings of
success, and yet who failed completely. To see a pop group's success
merely in terms of its hype and financial backing is extremely reductive
and does not allow for consumer choice, skill or charisma on the part
of the performers and so on.

8   Savage (1990, p. 155) makes the point that '[w]hat is then ignored in
most accounts of consumer capitalism is the way in which consuming
can be an active as well as a passive choice, or in this context how
people can use pop music'. He is referring specifically to the way in
which gay imagery is used in the hyping and selling of ostensibly
straight pop. This gay imagery may well be read as non-gay by non-
gay audiences, but it is likely that the group from whom the imagery
was taken (basically gay men) will make different readings of the same
range of signs and symbols, that they will understand the messages in
different, more group-specific ways.

9   The meanings here are complex and are out of the scope of this essay, but further work in this area could prove extremely productive.
10 The architect Charles Jencks invented and first used the term and only intended it in its limited architectural sense.
11 Ellis (1989, p. 13) makes a similar point with regard to Derrida, but it could equally well apply to any of the postmodern and post-structuralist theorists.

References

Baudrillard, J. (1981), *For a Critique of the Political Economy of the Sign*, trans. Charles Levin (St Louis, Mo.).

Benjamin, W. (1977), 'The Work of Art in the Age of Mechanical Reproduction' in J. Curran, M. Gurevitch and J. Woollacott ed., *Mass Communication and Society* (London), pp. 384–408.

Bordwell, D., Staiger, J. and Thompson, K. (1985), *The Classical Hollywood Cinema* (London).

Bronski, M. (1984), *Culture Clash – the Making of Gay Sensibility* (Boston, Mass.) (particularly the chapter 'Movies: Hollywood Homo-sense', pp. 92–109).

Dyer, R. (1982), 'A Star is Born and the Construction of Authenticity' in *Star Signs – Papers from a Weekend Workshop* (London).

Ellis, J. M. (1989), *Against Deconstruction* (Princeton, N.J.).

Goodwin, A. (1990), 'Sample and Hold: Pop Music in the Digital Age of Reproduction' in A. Goodwin and S. Frith ed., *On Record: Rock, Pop and the Written Word* (New York), pp. 258–73.

Hayes, Joseph J. (1981), 'Gay speak' in James W. Chesebro ed., *Gayspeak: Gay Male and Lesbian Communication* (New York), pp. 49–57.

Hebdige, D. (1979), *Subculture: the Meaning of Style* (London).

Hebdige, D. (1987), *Cut 'N' Mix: Culture, Identity and Caribbean Music* (London).

Hebdige, D. (1989), 'After the Masses', *Marxism Today* (January), pp. 48–53.

Itkonen, E. (1988), 'A Critique of the Post-structuralist Conception of Language', *Semiotica*, vol. 71, nos 3/4, pp. 305–20.

Jameson, F. 'Postmodernism, or The Cultural Logic of Late Capitalism', *New Left Review*; no. 146 (August 1984), pp. 53–92.

Lash, S. and Urry, J. (1987), *The End of Organized Capitalism* (Cambridge).

Rimmer, D. (1985), *Like Punk Never Happened: Culture Club and the New Pop* (London).

Sampson, Edward E. (1989), 'Foundations for a Textual Analysis of Selfhood' in J. Shotter and K. Gergen eds., *Texts of Identity* (London), pp. 1–19.

Savage, J. (1990), 'Tainted Love: The Influence of Male Homosexuality and Sexual Divergence on Pop Music and Culture since the War' in A. Tomlinson ed., *Consumption, Identity, and Style* (London), pp. 153–71.

Derek Scott

Sexuality and musical style from Monteverdi to Mae West

This chapter examines some of the conventions involved in representing sexuality in music, and considers how musical style may be related to ideology. The disparity revealed by comparing representations of sexual desire in three differing musical styles (Baroque opera, the Victorian drawing-room ballad and popular music of the 1920s and 1930s in the USA) shows that a genealogy of sexuality in music needs to address disjunctions rather than developments, historical rather than evolutionary questions.

Representations of gender in music are not restricted to erotic sexuality; it would be possible to devote an essay to a discussion of how musical representations of male and female laughter differ, or to a comparison of male and female grief. However, for want of space, I have chosen eroticism – if that is not too strong a word to describe my Victorian examples – because it offers clear examples of how gender difference is constructed in music. And what we find here are disjunctions in representation rather than any kind of universals or constants that can be traced through the changes brought about by an autonomous evolution or 'progress' of musical style. There is certainly no progress to be discovered in the way sexuality has been depicted in music: representations of sexuality in contemporary music are not more 'real' now than they were in the seventeenth century. The fact that the latter can seem alien to us now points to the way sexuality has been constructed in relation to particular stylistic codes in particular historical contexts and is therefore cultural rather than natural.

It may already be accepted that everyday notions of sexuality are socially constructed rather than a reflection of the natural world. Indeed, we may follow Julia Kristeva in regarding the categories of masculine and feminine as metaphysical; but, in the light of the foregoing remarks, it does not follow from this acceptance that music acts as a simple channel through which ideologies of gender are mediated and may be renegotiated. In other words, *sexual ideology cannot be straightforwardly renegotiated in music, because a representation of sexuality in music has to relate to the pre-given code of the particular musical style within which it is articulated.*

Certain popular musical styles, though, have sometimes been treated as if they had arisen from attempts to negotiate differing *expressions* of sexuality in music. In their study of 'Rock and Sexuality' (1978), Simon Frith and Angela McRobbie have a tendency to see the bifurcation of rock into what they call 'cock' rock and 'soft' rock in these terms. John Shepherd, too, makes the point that 'notions of gender and "sexuality" can be renegotiated by "popular" musicians', adding, 'Negotiation is the key concept in understanding how the politically personal is articulated from within the internal process of music' (1987, 172). Roland Barthes's essay 'The Grain of the Voice' (1977), a frequent departure point for considerations of the radical possibilities of timbre (though Barthes's 'grain' is not synonymous with timbre), encourages Shepherd to theorise about the potentialities of female timbres within a male musical hegemony. Yet, while it is argued that timbre is an arena for negotiation in 'popular' music, vocal timbre is apparently regarded as a fixed, ideologically-encoded parameter in 'classical' music. Nevertheless, not only have 'classical' timbres changed remarkably even in our own century (what alto today sings with the timbre of Dame Clara Butt?), but particular timbres have, by way of contrast, been long established features of some 'popular' styles (for example, the high, 'lonesome' tenor of Appalachian music still to be heard in contemporary bluegrass).

With the above in mind it is clear that a song like Tammy Wynette's 'Stand by Your Man' (Wynette–Sherill) cannot be fully understood solely in terms of its being an *expression* in music (negotiated or otherwise) of the ideology of supportive and sub-missive femininity, but must also be considered in relation to the stylistic expectations and constraints of 1960s Nashville country music. This is why Billie Holiday sounds so different when 'standing by *her* man' in songs like 'Don't Explain' (Holiday–Herzog). One singer is not offering a more 'real' submission than the other, but a different musical discourse of submission. In the words of Jenny

Taylor and Dave Laing, what is at issue is 'the radically different codes and conventions of representation involved in different genres' (1979, 46).

Given that representations of female sexuality are constructed within particular musical styles, and that musical styles are signifying practices, it is evident, as deconstructionists have shown, that what is being signified is 'up for grabs' (something the recent lesbian appropriation of country and western has demonstrated). You may feel convinced that something is a reflection of reality if, in Althusserian terms, its ideological character has interpellated (or hailed) you as a subject, but history has a way of slowly revealing the ideological character of representations. Readers of appropriate age may like to weigh up how camp Mick Jagger appears today in film shot in the 1960s, and how wild and sexy he seemed at the time. Here, I am considering how differing musical idioms represent sexuality – from Poppea's 'O mio ben, o mio cor, o mio tesoro' to Mae West's 'Oh, oh, oh'. Along the way we have three things to consider:

A. How does a composer represent sexuality?

B. How does a performer convey sexuality?

C. How does a listener interpret sexuality (e.g. interpret a performance as erotic, or 'read' a female composition as feminine)?

Taking the case of eroticism and music we can see how the possibilities and complexities of this relationship increase as we move from one to another of the above questions.

There are two possibilities to bear in mind in relation to A: either the composer has encoded eroticism or *not* (as text). There are three possibilities to consider in relation to B: the performer conveys sexuality by decoding the eroticism in the text of the composition, *or* adds eroticism and encodes the result in sound (timbre), *or* there is no eroticism yet. When we turn to C there are four possibilities: the listener decodes eroticism in the composition but finds the performer unerotic, *or* finds the performer's voice erotic but the composition not, *or* finds both erotic (decodes at two levels), *or* 'reads' eroticism where there is none (perhaps because of expectation). In the case of the listener who finds the performer's voice erotic but the composition not, the *jouissance* of the non-signifying genosong may be said to have obliterated the communicative structure of the phenosong; in other words the signified is ignored in favour of the sensually-produced meaning Barthes calls *signifiance*. The terms 'genotext' and 'phenotext' were coined by Kristeva (1974), but adroitly applied to music by Barthes as 'genosong' and 'phenosong' (1977, 182). The listener who finds the performer physically erotic, but neither the performer's voice nor the composition erotic, may still be displaying a cultural response, but can be eliminated on the grounds that such a response has nothing to do with the subject of *musical style* under discussion here.

The present study of representations of sexuality begins in the seventeenth century. This was a time, according to Michel Foucault, when the transformation of sexuality into discourse which began in the preceding century was completed:

First the Reformation, then tridentine Catholicism, mark an important mutation and a schism in what might be called the 'traditional technology of the flesh.' A division whose depth should not be underestimated; but this did not rule out a certain parallelism in the Catholic and Protestant methods of examination of conscience and pastoral direction: procedures for analyzing 'concupiscence' and transforming it into discourse were established in both instances. (Foucault 1981, 116)

Although the sixteenth century was not lacking in ability to represent affective states, as the Netherlands motet shows (see Meyer 1956, 219), it was in seventeenth-century music that a *stile rappresentativo* was consciously established. This development in representational techniques has been described by Susan McClary as a 'tangle of gender, rhetoric and power' (McClary 1990, 223). Unlike Jacques Attali, who identifies the period of representation in music history as beginning in the eighteenth century with the rise of the musical commodity as spectacle (1985, 81), McClary proposes that it was 'ushered in with great fanfare with the invention of opera, monody, and sonata in the first decade of the seventeenth century' (1985, 154).

In Baroque opera the problem may arise of a lack of recognition of a representation of eroticism by the composer. Such would be the case where the composer's music was found to be petrified: the only aesthetic titillation Carl Dahlhaus was willing to concede might be found in Monteverdi's music was related entirely to its remoteness in history (1982, 98). This problem may be solved by an editor, an arranger or a performer. For example, in the 1960s when it was considered dramatically unacceptable for a woman to

sing the castrato role of Nero in *L'incoronazione di Poppea* (1642), it
was common for the part to be sung an octave lower by a man.
That was done, in spite of its effect on the actual music (sometimes
inverting dissonances, for example), in order to conform to audience
expectations of male operatic sexuality. Worries about Poppea's
music not being found sexy enough were solved by 'tarting up'
the instrumentation, and ensuring Poppea's personal wardrobe (or
the lack of it) absorbed the masculine gaze. Producers of this
opera found themselves in a contrary position to those involved in
Wagnerian music drama, where it was accepted that eroticism
would often be recognised in the music but not in the performer.

We will now consider the Nero/Poppea duet 'Pur ti miro' as a
representation in music of the mutual arousal thought necessary for
sexual reproduction in the seventeenth century (Ex. 1). The idea
that both men and women needed to ejaculate seed lies behind the
following advice given by the surgeon Ambroise Paré:

When the husband commeth into his wives chamber hee must entertaine
her with all kinde of dalliance, wanton behaviour, and allurements to
venery: but if he perceive her to be slow, and more cold, he must cherish,
embrace, and tickle her, and shall not abruptly, the nerves being suddenly
distended, breake into the field of nature, but rather shall creepe in by
little and little intermixing more wanton kisses with wanton words and
speeches, handling her secret parts and dugs, that she may take fire and
bee enflamed to venery, for so at length the wombe will strive and waxe
fervent with a desire of casting forth its owne seed, and receiving the
mans seed to bee mixed together therewith. (*The Workes of that Famous
Chirurgian Ambrose Parey*, trans. Thomas Johnson, London: Thomas
Cotes, 1634, p. 889, quoted in Greenblatt 1988, 180)

Since this duet is now thought not to be by Monteverdi, though
once readily accepted as such, it will go some way to illustrating
musical conventions (which in themselves are ideological constructs)
without, perhaps, our being so readily sidetracked into questions of
artistic genius. Moreover, as Margaret Murata has argued, there
was something of an oral character to Western seventeenth-century
music, evidenced by its common pool of musical materials (1988).
Susan McClary has discussed how the seventeenth-century concern
for mutual arousal may be perceived in music, and here we certainly
have an example of her two equal voices rubbing up against each
other 'pressing into dissonances that achingly resolve only into yet
other knots, reaching satiety only at conclusions' (1990, 206). The

(Ex. 1)

(Ex. 2)

rapid exchanges of the middle section form a neat example, too, of the stimulating 'friction to heat' that Stephen Greenblatt has suggested lies behind the erotic repartee in Shakespearian comedy (1988, 89–90). We are more used to Nero's pitch now (thanks to the familiarity of high male voices in early music performances and the high falsetto in popular music associated with performers like the Bee Gees), but can we recapture the significance of that male pitch for the seventeenth-century audience? Was it *intended* to sound unnatural, in the sense of befitting a god or someone more than ordinarily human?

Cleopatra's aria 'V'adoro pupille', from Handel's opera *Giulio Cesare in Egitto* (1724) (Ex. 2) contains short phrases suggestive of breathlessness as in the above; but note Cleopatra's rhetorical skill – the way she is able to extend a phrase unexpectedly and to wind Caesar into her musical embrace. At every point where we expect closure the line continues, clinging on to Caesar and allowing him no opportunity to interrupt or escape. She takes the lead in their relationship, yet to Caesar 'her bold courtship [is] taken as passive yearning' (Hughes-Hallet 1991, 209). Rising sequences are also used in this aria to suggest erotic stimulus, as in the previous duet. The instrumentation is unusual: it includes a harp which may be regarded as substituting for the lyre, the instrument of the erotic muse, Erato. Poppea has the rhetorical skills of the courtesan, Cleopatra the rhetorical skill of the sovereign. In Monteverdi's *Orfeo*, Euridice has none, the sign of an 'innocent' young woman, as McClary has argued and demonstrated (1990, 211–15).

The second 'especially productive moment' in the proliferation of sexual discourse is located by Foucault in the nineteenth century with 'the advent of medical technologies of sex' (1981, 119). The nineteenth century witnessed the development of a 'completely new technology of sex':

Through pedagogy, medicine, and economics, it made sex not only a secular concern but a concern of the state as well; to be more exact, sex became a matter that required the social body as a whole, and virtually all of its individuals, to place themselves under surveillance. (1981, 116)

'Won't You Tell Me Why, Robin?' by Claribel (1861) is as close as we get to a seduction song from female to male in a Victorian drawing-room ballad, the content being full of delicately phrased hints, pleas and accusations (Ex. 3). The use of a diminished seventh chord exchanging with the tonic (a non-functional colouristic effect), is a Romantic device employed earlier by Haydn (slow movement of Symphony no. 104), and still around to provide a romantic *frisson* in Cole Porter's 'True Love'. There are short phrases again, but here they do not suggest breathlessness, rather decorous restraint, a sign, perhaps, that the singer has 'placed herself under surveillance'. The 6/8 rhythm is a pastoral convention inherited from the eighteenth century befitting the rural setting, but the song is for an urban market, so there is an element of

1. You are not what you were, Rob-in; Why so sad and strange? You once were blithe and gay, Rob-in; What has made you change? You

2. On Sun-day af-ter church, Rob-in, I look'd a-round for you; I thought you'd see me home, Rob-in, As once you used to do; But

3. The oth-er night we danc'd, Rob-in, Be-neath the haw-thorn tree, I thought you'd sure-ly come, Rob-in If but to dance with me; But

(Ex. 3)

(Ex. 4)

fantasy present. This ballad offers itself as a possible vehicle for drawing-room flirtation behind a mask of otherness, just as songs of Arcadian nymphs and shepherds subtly underlined from a respectful distance the use of Vauxhall Gardens for courtship. Robin was a name not without sexual connotations in the nineteenth century, sometimes explicitly phallic, as in 'Colin and Susan' ('A famous New Smutty Song') published in an erotic songbook of the 1830s (reprinted in Waites and Hunter 1984, 65).

It is obvious from the style of 'Only' by Virginia Gabriel (1871) that a man is admiring a woman, even though the words of the first verse make no reference to either sex (however, 'angel' in the last line, which would automatically have had feminine connotations for most Victorian listeners, begins to give the game away). Here, a woman composer is adopting a 'thrusting' style to represent male ardour (Ex. 4). A vigorous rhythm on alternating tonics and dominants would have associations with such things as timpani parts in martial music; it would connote power and boldness, activity rather than passivity, in other words masculinity rather than femininity. But was it appropriate for a Victorian woman composer to write this sort of music?

As more and more women took to composition, nineteenth-century criticism moved away from the use of 'masculine' and 'feminine' as metaphors in describing music towards their solidification into an aesthetic confirmation of sexual difference. It is interesting to note that this aesthetic development coincides with the emergence of a *scientia sexualis* (see Foucault 1981, 68). From the metaphorical use of these terms, a practice which in characterising some music by men as 'feminine' offered the possibility of 'masculine' music by women, 'the language of Romantic music criticism degenerated into a language of sexual aesthetics, in which the potentialities of the individual female composer were defined through the application of sexual stereotypes' (Tick 1986, 336). It came to be interpreted as a failing for a woman to seek to write 'masculine' music, and she 'received much advice to cultivate art from the feminine stand-point' (Stratton 1883, 131). The 'feminine' in music was 'charming', 'sweet', 'delicate', 'sensitive', etc., and women songwriters were to offer work that was 'pretty', 'charming', 'adorable', etc., i.e. work which could be labelled or thought of in ways distinct from male creativity. The drawing-room ballad came to be thought an ideal outlet for female compositional creativity in the 1860s because even its performance associations were feminine: 'The preference for the English ballad is easily accounted for: the melody is not uncommonly very pretty, the words are understood, and every repetition of it in any form recalls the touching voice and the pretty face of the singer from whom we first heard it' (Macdonell 1860, 384).

Yet, though the musical style of 'Only' is clearly gendered, it characterises the male in love in contrast to the female in love. Its reception, therefore, would have been problematic because of its having been composed by a woman. It would have been seen not as an example of a woman successfully challenging a male composer on his own ground (as we may be tempted to view it today), but as an example of 'a striking reproduction of masculine art', as one critic described Alice Smith's composition *The Passions* in 1882 (cited by Stratton, 128). The ability to reproduce, rather than originate, was held to be a peculiarity of the female mind. If a woman's temperament was deemed 'naturally artistic', those words were to be understood 'not in a creative, but in a receptive sense' (Haweis 1871, 102). Sexual aesthetics were part of 'separate spheres' ideology: Ruskin, for example, had proclaimed in his lecture *Of Queens' Gardens* in 1864 that a woman's intellect was 'not for invention or creation, but for sweet ordering, arrangement, and decision' (Ruskin 1907, 59). It is important to recognise that there was nothing conspiratorial in such statements, but that, once formulated, these ideas were understood as truths always and already present.

The musical style representing a jilted male or a male pleading with the female object of his desire is similarly gendered. 'Come into the Garden, Maud' (Tennyson–Balfe, 1857) is a plea to a beloved, like 'Won't You Tell Me Why, Robin?'. There is a well-known anecdote that tells how Marie Lloyd made this song sound indecent when she sang it during a court case to prove that 'filth' was in the mind. But it is, perhaps, difficult today to understand how *easy* it would have been for a woman to make it sound indecent, something that would have been accomplished effortlessly then because the song's musical style conforms to a Victorian representation of virile *male* sexuality. That passionate conclusion is utterly unseemly for the ideal submissive 'perfect lady' of Victorian times. And yet, the song amuses now (especially the conclusion), thus providing another example of disjunction in representational codes. So much for an expression of 'real' eroticism.

Finally, we come to the early twentieth century which, for Foucault, was characterised by a deployment of sexuality 'spread through the entire social body' (1981, 122), the birth of the 'theory of repression' (1981, 128), and the emergence of psychoanalysis in response (1981, 129). Three female stereotypes dominate American songs of the 1920s and 1980s: one is the Predator (she'll get men); a second is the Innocent (she's available and doesn't know what she's doing); and a third is the Prim and Proper. The last is more difficult to describe: she may be a school teacher, or a secretary in tweeds wearing severe glasses which, when removed, cause the astonished male to gulp, 'But . . . you're beautiful!' Or she may be in uniform (particularly of a military or religious kind), a woman whose sexual feelings need to be 'awakened' by a strong man who will reassure her and calm her fear of those 'repressed' feelings. Her potentially seething passion is kept in check by her strict moral code (itself evidence of 'repressed desire'). These three are not the only possible stereotypes of female sexuality, of course, but they were the ones favoured in the USA at this time. By way of contrast, in Germany there was the indolent or languid sensuality of Marlene Dietrich, and in England there was the 'saucy local gal' in the tradition of Marie Lloyd. A stereotype is a representation repeated as if it were natural, or a known constant. It is an imitation 'no longer sensed as an imitation' (Barthes 1990, 42). In other words, the danger of a stereotype is that it may come to be misrecognised as 'truth': 'Nietzsche has observed that 'truth' is only the solidification of old metaphors. So in this regard the stereotype is the present path of 'truth,' the palpable feature which shifts the invented ornament to the canonical, constraining form of the signified' (Barthes 1990, 42–3). We have already seen how metaphors of masculinity and femininity solidified into truth in the nineteenth century.

In 'I Like a Guy What Takes His Time' (Rainger), recorded in New York early in 1933, Mae West is cast in the predator/dominatrix category (this and the other American songs of the 1920s and 1930s mentioned below are available on the BBC recording *The Classic Years in Digital Stereo: Saucy Songs*, ZCF 728, 1989). She was, incidentally, a lion tamer in the film *I'm No Angel* later that same year. Prominence is given to West's erotic moaning, but other erotic devices of the time, for example, the Sophie Tucker or Bessie Smith growl, or the heavy breathing of Ethel Waters (compare the latter's 1930 recording of the Fain–

Norman song 'You Brought a New Kind of Love to Me'), play no part. In this context, West's Brooklyn accent and nasal delivery would have carried suggestions of low life and loose morality. The change to double time, which elsewhere would have been simply a characteristic jazz technique, operates in this song as a humorous reference to the amateur lover who does not 'take his time'.

In 'Come up and See Me Sometime' (Swanstrom–Alter), recorded in New York in 1933. Cliff Edwards's voice sounds camp, and intentionally so for there is no other way a man can handle this kind of Mae West material (West did not record this song, but it is clearly indebted to her performances in style and content). Marybeth Hamilton suggests that West's style 'would have resonated with a 1930s gay sensibility', and observes that 'exaggerated speech and mannerisms had already begun to be labelled "camp" in the 1920s' (1990, 225–6). The dominant culture did not permit a 'real man' to indulge in techniques associated with the supposed seductive skills of women. Cliff Edwards, in fact, is faced with the same problem (how to exhibit eroticism as a man) that McClary sees as hampering the eponymous character in Monteverdi's *Orfeo* (1990, 220).

In 'Is There Anything Wrong in That?' (Magidson–Cleary), recorded in New York in 1928, Helen Kane plays the 'innocent abroad', or 'dumb blonde' stereotype. The trumpet, played with wow-wow mute, is intended to be both sexy and comic, like the song, and like Kane's voice which it resembles. We do not know, in fact, which is imitating which, an ambiguity of considerable importance to the development of a purely instrumental erotic code in dance-band music of this period.

In 'Pu-Leeze! Mister Hemingway' (Drake–Kent–Silver), re-corded in London in 1932, Ann Suter portrays the 'prim but pliable' stereotype, the woman who has to be conquered by the male. There are elements of sado-masochism present: the record concludes with a resounding slap as she fights off the libidinous Mr Hemingway.

Mae West and others playing the predatory stereotype appro-priated the smears, bent notes, and growling plunger-mute effects of the Cotton Club in Harlem. There, Duke Ellington, aided by trumpeter Bubber Miley and trombonist Joe Nanton, satisfied the expectations of their white patrons by serving up such effects as 'jungle music' (Ellington sometimes recorded under the pseudonym

'The Jungle Band'). Hence, associations of the wild and the primitive pass over to the singer utilising these devices. Then, becoming associated with representations of wild, predatory female sexuality, these effects (which are now heard as female cries, purrs, moans, groans and breathless gasps) can return as a highly-charged yet non-vocal musical eroticism. In a well-known later piece, David Rose's 'The Stripper' (1962), note the quasi-vocal slides on trombone and the wailing *tremolando* on a blue seventh followed by 'jungle' drums. Yet compare this with another discursive code, Richard Strauss's *Salome* (1905), which Ernst Krause claims 'established the modern musical formula for the portrayal of ecstatic sensual desire and brought it to perfection' (1974, n.p.). The eroticism of the 'Dance of the Seven Veils' is encoded in the sensual richness (timbral and textural) of a huge orchestra, the quasi-oriental (i.e. exotic) embellishment of melody, and the devices of *crescendo* and quickening pace. However, it is no coincidence that, despite the anachronism, the Viennese waltz with its connotations of *fin de siècle* decadence lies just below the surface of the Strauss, as the fox trot lies below that of the Rose. There is no sense, of course, in which one is really sexier than the other; each encodes eroticism in a different way and for a different function. It would be just as ludicrous to imagine Strauss's 'Dance of the Seven Veils' in a seedy strip club as to imagine Rose's 'The Stripper' incorporated into *Salome*. There *is* no perfect musical portrayal of 'ecstatic sensual desire' independent of sociocultural context. Rose's piece sounds like camp eroticism now, and seems to confirm the idea of a new erotic era beginning the following year. As Larkin put it memorably in his poem 'Annus Mirabilis'.

> Sexual intercourse began
> In nineteen sixty-three
> (Which was rather late for me) –
> Between the end of the *Chatterley* ban
> And the Beatles' first LP.   (Larkin 1974, 34)

Is this partly why Mae West now sounds camp – because these timbres have become clichés?

In the early 1930s Mae West did represent a sexuality which many felt reflected a 'real' sexuality. Indeed, she served a prison sentence in 1927 for *SEX*, a play which critics implied 'was no theatrical representation of a brothel, but . . . uncomfortably resembled a real one' (Hamilton 1990, 56). Even when West began to mediate her sexuality through a historical setting (to avoid charges of literally transporting New York's sexual underworld to the Broadway stage), her representation of late nineteenth-century low life was thought authentic. Consideration, of course, needs to be given to the question of how far West began to introduce self-parody into her performances of the 1930s. These performances were certainly ambiguous, allowing her ironic detachment to be read as parody. Hamilton, however, claims that in the early 1930s West 'understood her "irony" as simply a suggestive inflection, a means of hinting that more was going on than lay on the surface, a vague something whose exact substance she never made clear' (1990, 270). The Legion of Decency, campaigning for movie reform in 1933–4, failed to recognise irony, parody or comedy of any kind in West's performances, and considered her a moral threat to young women (see Hamilton 1990, 240–1). It was after 1934, to appease the Production Code Administration, that West was obliged to provide an unambiguous mediation of her sexuality, one which would be perceived as non-threatening because recognised as unreal. As we noted above, however, Cliff Edwards in imitating her only ever had the option, as a man, of sounding unreal. It seems that male and female representations of sexuality can occupy the same terrain only when one or the other of them is the 'cod' version. In this connection we may note Ellie Ragland-Sullivan's words in elucidation of Lacan's phallic signifier:

Feminine sexuality – not necessarily correlated with gender – is a masquerade not only because s/he can disguise her desire, can fake it, can cover her body with cosmetics and jewels and make of *it* a phallus, but also because her masquerade hides a fact – that masculine sexuality is a tenuous matter. Things do not work so easily between man and woman, or between any sexual partners for that matter. If *only* this point were understood, Lacan's phallic signifier would not be read imaginarily – i.e. essentialized – as a privileging of the masculine. It would be seen rather, as a dividing effect created by learning difference as gender difference. (1991, 71)

When Mick Jagger was thought to reflect an unbridled male sexuality there were no female imitators of his style. By the late 1980s, when those old Stones records were sounding camp, Annie Lennox was able to appropriate the style in a song like 'I Need a Man' (Lennox–Stewart, 1987). The difference between this and

Mae West and Cliff Edwards is that performances by the last
two were contemporaneous, whereas Lennox is quoting a style of
representation that has become historic. It is the historic character
of the quotation that helps to make the latter case an example of
the postmodern. The 'dominatrix' and 'innocent' stereotypes of
Hollywood femininity discussed above are deliberately quoted in
songs by Madonna, which is partly what makes her a postmodern
artist. The other usual requirement of the postmodern (which
Lennox and Madonna both seem aware of) is that it should be
double coded: a quotation may serve merely to inscribe, but a
sense of parody or self-consciousness about a quotation can serve
additionally to subvert.

Parody in postmodern art is more than just a sign of the attention artists
pay to each others' work and to the art of the past. It may indeed be
complicitous with the values it inscribes as well as subverts, but the
subversion is still there. (Hutcheon 1989, 106)

I would argue, however, that authorial intention is not essential for
postmodern subversion to work; subversion can occur in reception
and interpretation (no postmodernist would accept a servile position
towards a text). A single example must suffice by way of illustra-
tion, since there is no space here to engage with the critique of the
self-present subject, post-structuralist arguments concerning the
incompleteness of all texts, or the concept of 'différance' which
Jacques Derrida has used to designate 'the production of differing/
deferring' (1974, 23). When Kate Bush quotes the innocent girlish
voice in her song 'Wuthering heights', our reception may be
coloured by a knowledge of the novel, where the little girl's plea to
be let in at the window is answered with misogynistic violence.
Such a response does not reply upon Bush's intended meaning,
whatever that may have been.

References

Attali, Jacques (1985), *Noise: The Political Economy of Music*, trans. Brian
    Massumi (Manchester) (first published 1977).
Barthes, Roland (1977), 'The Grain of the Voice', trans. Stephen Heath in
    Barthes, *Image–Music–Text*, (London) pl. 179–89, reprinted in Frith
    and Goodwin (1990), pp. 293–300.

Barthes, Roland (1990), *The Pleasure of the Text*, trans. Richard Miller (Oxford) (first published 1973).

Dahlhaus, Carl (1982), *Esthetics of Music*, trans. William Austin (Cambridge) (first published 1967).

Derrida, Jacques (1974), *Of Grammatology*, trans. Gayatri Chakravorty Spivak (London).

Foucault, Michel (1981), *The History of Sexuality: Vol. 1, An Introduction*, trans. Robert Hurley (Harmondsworth) (first published 1976).

Frith, Simon and Goodwin, Andrew, ed. (1990), *On Record: Rock, Pop, and the Written Word* (London).

Frith, Simon and McRobbie, Angela (1978), 'Rock and Sexuality', *Screen Education*, vol. 29, pp. 3–19, reprinted in Frith and Goodwin (1990), pp. 371–89.

Greenblatt, Stephen (1988), *Shakespearean Negotiations* (Oxford).

Hamilton, Marybeth (1990), 'When I'm Bad, I'm Better': Mae West and American Popular Entertainment', unpublished Ph.D. thesis, Princeton University.

Haweis, Hugh (1871), *Music and Morals*, reprint of 1871 edn (London).

Hughes-Hallet, Lucy (1991), *Cleopatra: Histories, Dreams and Distortions* (London).

Hutcheon, Linda (1989), *The Politics of Postmodernism* (London).

Krause, Ernst (1974), Notes, trans. Kenneth Howe, accompanying records *The Orchestral Music of Richard Strauss, Vol. 3*, HMV SLS 894, no pagination.

Kristeva, Julia (1974), *Revolution in Poetic Language*, trans. Margaret Waller (1984), extracts reprinted in Toril Moi, ed. (1986), *The Kristeva Reader* (Oxford), B. pp. 90–136.

Larkin, Philip (1974), *High Windows* (London).

McClary, Susan (1985), 'Afterword: The Politics of Silence and Sound', in Attali (1985), pp. 149–58.

McClary, Susan (1990), 'Constructions of Gender in Monteverdi's Dramatic Music', *Cambridge Opera Journal*, vol. 1, no. 3, pp. 203–23.

Macdonell, J. B. (1860), 'Classical Music and British Musical Taste', *Macmillan's Magazine*, vol. 1, pp. 383–9.

Meyer, Leonard B. (1956) *Emotion and Meaning in Music* (London).

Murata, Margaret (1988), 'Scylla and Charybdis, or Steering Between Form and Social Context in the Seventeenth Century' in Eugene Narmour and Ruth A. Solie, ed., *Explorations in Music, the Arts, and Ideas: Essays in Honor of Leonard B. Meyer* (Stuyvesant), pp. 67–85.

Ragland-Sullivan, Ellie (1991), 'The Sexual Masquerade: A Lacanian Theory of Sexual Difference' in Ellie Ragland-Sullivan and Mark Bracher, ed., *Lacan and the Subject of Language* (London), pp. 49–80.

Ruskin, John (1907), *Sesame & Lilies* (London) (first published 1865).

Shepherd, John (1987), 'Music and Male Hegemony' in Richard Leppert and Susan McClary, ed., *Music and Society: The Politics of Composition, Performance and Reception* (Cambridge), pp. 151–72.

Shepherd, John (1991), *Music as Social Text* (Cambridge).

Stratton, Stephen (1883), 'Women in Relation to Musical Art', *Proceedings of the Royal Musical Association*, vol. 9, pp. 125–31.

Taylor, Jenny and Laing, Dave (1979), 'Disco-Pleasure-Discourse: On "Rock and Sexuality"'. *Screen Education*, vol. 31, pp. 43–8.

Tick, Judith (1986), 'Passed Away Is the Piano Girl: Changes in American Musical Life, 1870–1900' in Jane Bowers and Judith Tick, ed., *Women Making Music: The Western Art Tradition, 1150–1950* (London), pp. 325–48.

Waites, Aline and Hunter, Robin (1984), *The Illustrated Victorian Songbook* (London).

Paul Théberge

Random access: music, technology, postmodernism

My earliest memory of music is not the sound of my mother's voice, although she may have sung to me when I was a small child; nor is it the sound of my grandfather's fiddle – by the time I was born he was quite old and had long since ceased to play. My earliest memories of music are the sounds (mostly rock and roll and sometimes opera) that came from a brown plastic radio that sat in my parents' kitchen, those from a small, box-like phonograph (recordings of children's songs and my parents' collection of Broadway musicals), and those from an even smaller transistor radio that I often carried to the beach. I remember occasionally seeing musicians play live but none made as big an impression on me as, when I was about ten years old, seeing the Beatles' television appearance on the Ed Sullivan Show; not long after, when I decided to take up my first musical instrument, it was not the fiddle, but the electric guitar. All these experiences seemed real enough to me at the time; it never occurred to me that musical culture was possible, or even desirable, without electronic technology.

Of course, my experiences were certainly not unique – just about everyone I knew seemed to be listening to the same things, responding to the same forces. And many years later, after having learned to read music and having assimilated a number of musical styles (including the music of several continents and so-called 'serious' music), after having learned to play (rather badly) a number of musical instruments, both electronic and acoustic (even the fiddle that once belonged to my grandfather), I find myself still feeling much the same way about technology: indeed, I am more sure than ever that electronic technologies, and the industries that supply them, are not simply the technical and economic context within which 'music' is made, but rather, they are among the very preconditions for contemporary musical culture, thought of in its broadest sense, in the latter half of the twentieth century. One need not celebrate technology to realise that our experience of electronic technologies – microphones and electric guitars; amplification equipment in club, stadium or disco; multi-track studios and music computers; synthesisers, samplers and drum machines; background music systems, radio and television; records, cassette tapes and CDs; hi-fi systems, car stereos, ghetto blasters and 'Walkmen' – conditions our musical sensibilities (whether positively or negatively), influences our production and consumption practices, our aesthetic expectations and our notions of what constitutes music and musical expression.

But electronic technology is only one component in a complex economic, social and cultural phenomenon or 'condition' which has, over the past fifteen or twenty years, come to be known as 'postmodernity'. The precise contours of the phenomenon itself have been the subject of considerable debate throughout the 1980s but regardless of the various divergences of opinion, technology – as catalyst, metaphor, or background ideology – has been a common element in most accounts. It also figures prominently in a variety of cultural strategies – minimalist, feminist, Black and deconstructivist, among others – that have fallen (rightly or wrongly) under the general rubric of 'postmodernism'. I do not intend to summarise or debate the various theoretical and aesthetic arguments concerning postmodernity and postmodernism here or to take sides (although my affinities with certain positions will be obvious enough); instead, I will take a certain licence, 'sample' them whenever it seems appropriate, make them part of my own 'mix'.

In this chapter I shall be primarily concerned with two inter-related issues regarding the role of technology in the production and consumption of music in the postmodern era: firstly, I want to consider how the development of new technologies, in conjunction with organisational shifts in the music industry, has contributed to the formation of what might be considered as a postmodern sensibility and, secondly, I want to examine some of the characteristics of electronic and digital technology with regards to the technical production/reproduction of music. From time to time I will also pause to compare some of these postmodern attitudes and practices to earlier attitudes towards musical culture and to the technical practices of modernism.

Technology and 'global culture'

Musical experience in the postmodern era is anything but singular: it is, firstly, a highly mobile form of experience (the Sony 'Walkman' being only the most recent and seductive of a whole series of technologies whose only goal is to allow us to listen to music almost anywhere and at any time); one conditioned by Top 40 radio (and now music television) formats with their non-stop parade of multiple voices (and bodies), fragmented emotions, desires and subject postions; one that takes for granted an unprecedented access to music (and, with samplers, individual musical sounds) from all parts of the world and virtually all periods of history; and finally, one whose apparent technical command over the details of production and consumption offers a feeling of individual control that is strangely complemented, and contradicted, by a manipulative and highly organised set of institutions and practices whose reach is global in scope and power. In each of these instances, music has become as much a spatial experience as a temporal one. The general notion of postmodernity that I want to develop here is related to certain ideas concerning musical space and time that are at once acoustic, technical, cultural and economic. And at all levels – from micro to macro – these ideas are related to issues of technology and technical/cultural form.

The development and diffusion of electronic technologies in music during the twentieth century has been extremely complex: generally speaking, the introduction of new inventions has been preceded by a long period in which scientific knowledge, technical practices, musical needs and marketing strategies are defined and developed in particular ways and within specific social groups; once introduced, however, these new technologies have become part of a social process in which new uses are defined by different social groups with different needs and interests. The ultimate significance of any technological development is thus neither singular, immediate nor entirely predictable.

Magnetic tape recording is a case in point. While the first prototype magnetic recorder was developed as early as 1898 and wire and steel-band magnetic recorders found limited use in radio broadcasting during the 1930s, it was not until 1948 that the first commercially successful tape machines were introduced. These machines found their first important uses in radio and record production where the overall improvement in sound fidelity, duration of recording time and, above all, the ability to edit and splice together different 'takes' of a performance contributed to a new flexibility in recording. The ease and relatively low cost of production also contributed to the rise of independent, entrepreneurial producers and a reorganisation of the recording industry. In contrast, consumer tape recording was relatively insignificant throughout the 1950s and early 1960s.

The most significant impact of tape recording, however, at least in terms of the arguments concerning postmodernism that will be pursued below, came only in the 1960s and early 1970s. Firstly, multi-track recording was adopted in popular music production, transforming the very basis of popular music practice, calling into question the validity of past notions of musical composition and performance, and creating new discontinuities in space and time unlike those of the early recording medium. During the 1970s, consumer multi-track equipment was introduced and, by the 1980s, the technology had become so pervasive that many computer programmers adopted a simulated version of multi-track tape recorder functions as the basis of the user interface for various computer-music applications.

Secondly, during the 1970s, inexpensive, portable cassette machines achieved a diffusion throughout the world that was unprecedented by any other music technology and they have become the basis of an emergent, worldwide popular music culture, on the one hand, and a vital element in the survival of local, regional and national music styles, on the other. Furthermore, because cassettes allow consumers to record as well as play back music, these various music cultures cannot be completely controlled by international corporate interests.

The discourse concerning cassette tape in the industrialised world has been dominated by transnational record companies seeking taxes and blank tape levies from national governments as financial compensation for losses due (or so they claim) to home taping. But quite apart from domestic consumer practices the cassette tape has been the basis of a variety of popular cultural strategies operating at street level: for example, long before samplers became

available, New York's Hip Hop culture had adopted cassette
recorders as a means of 'borrowing' material from radio and records,
editing and remixing it for their own purposes (and violating international copyright laws in the process); cassette tapes were also a
means of distribution – they fuelled the ghetto blasters that, in
turn, fuelled the street culture (Hebdige 1987, 141). Motti Regev
(1986) has shown how, not unlike early Hip Hop culture, marginal-
ized forms of Arab and Israeli popular musics developed their own
local distribution network through the use of cassette tapes; the
medium also became a prime means of 'musical street fighting'
in an attempt to establish a presence in a musical soundscape
dominated by the sounds of state and commercial radio. Wallis and
Malm (1984) have documented, in a variety of countries throughout the world, the diverse uses of cassette technology: from
guarantor of freedom of speech under repressive regimes to the
operations of large-scale commercial pirates who eat into the international profits of the record industry. And Jon Pareles has
described a vast, worldwide subculture of independent musicians
who use the cassette as their primary means of distribution (Pareles
1987). These diverse uses of the cassette tape recorder would
suggest that the power of *répétition*, which Jacques Attali (1977) has
argued was the essential nature of the political economy brought
into existence by technologies of mass reproduction, is not (or is no
longer) as monolithic as he and other critics would have us believe.

Thus, it could perhaps be argued that the present state of
affairs in the world of music and recent attitudes towards production and consumption have roots that date back at least to the 1950s
with changes in recording technology, aesthetics and other factors
that attained major cultural significance only much later. One of
the effects of magnetic tape mentioned above, in conjunction with
the introduction of the long-playing record (in 1948), was to increase
significantly the duration of musical recordings (the duration of 78
RPM recordings was approximately four minutes maximum). This
was not a mere quantitative change but also a qualitative one
in so far as it allowed a vast range of musical repertoire to be
recorded for the first time – a phenomenon that should not be
underestimated.

In the past, people's knowledge of the musical world – their
musical 'maps' – have always been defined and limited by history,
geography, ethnicity, social class and other factors. Certainly,

contact between cultures and musical assimilation has occured in the past but contact has often been sporadic and musical change relatively slow: for example, the orientalisms found in the music of Debussy and other composers is the result of brief encounters between European and colonial musicians that would only later became more frequent and of greater depth; and the profound outpouring of Afro-American music in the twentieth century could only have taken place after generations of acculturation. Initially, sound recording did not change this very much: although the phonograph and gramophone companies established operations throughout the world during the first decade of this century, recordings were primarily produced for local markets; in the United States, even Black music was initially sold in separate catalogues and in separate shops from other types of music.

The impact of the introduction of the tape recorder and LP may have been first felt, oddly enough, within the field of ethnomusicology. Since the 1950s, vast new collections of music from around the world have been made available through the efforts of ethnomusicologists themselves and the activities of commercial record companies. Bruno Nettl has suggested that the availability of so many recordings may have been a factor contributing to a shift of emphasis within the field during the postwar period – a shift away from the study of musical style through the detailed transcription of individual pieces of music (which was characteristic of the earlier period of archival recordings) towards the more general, anthropological approach to the study of musical behaviour (Nettl 1964, 24). (At the same time, commercial recording companies adopted a new attitude towards the recording of obscure repertoires of European art music of the distant past and initiated large recording projects aimed at establishing comprehensive catalogues of the works of important composers; Gould 1966, 50.)

This growth in the diversity of recordings was complemented by a growth in ethnomusicology as a discipline of study during the 1950s in the United States, State Department-sponsored tours by American musicians in developing countries during the 1960s, and changing relations between the European powers and their former colonies as the result of independence movements throughout the world. The impact of these and other events on musicians has been significant: jazz musicians such as John Coltrane and Don Cherry incorporated African and other non-Western elements into their

music during the 1960s; composers such as Lou Harrison freely
mix compositional procedures ranging from medieval to contemporary European music along with African and Asian musical traditions; and the entire minimalist school of composers of the 1960s
and 1970s has been heavily influenced by non-Western music. Of
the latter group, Steve Reich has been especially indebted to a
number of traditions through a series of brief encounters with
African, Indonesian and Middle Eastern musics.

During this same period, and in contrast to the early decades
of this century, the recording industry has moved towards an
increasingly integrated form of cultural production and marketing.
Roger Wallis and Krister Malm have described this strategy as one
in which small countries are regarded by the music industry as
potential sources of new talent and, also, as marginal markets
for mainstream recorded product (1984, xiii). The international
popularity of reggae music during the 1970s was perhaps the first
manifestation of this phenomenon. A factor that contributed to the
popularity of reggae was the fact that the music itself was a mixture
of African traditions and American pop music influences derived
from the spread of mass media.

The uses of recording technology established in reggae during
the 1960s and 1970s were quite unique; indeed, in many ways, the
form was dependent on technology (for financial reasons, reggae
was seldom performed live in Jamaica but was instead entirely
dependent on a network of recording studios and mobile dance
DJs). In the recording studio, engineers routinely began making
different mixes, or 'versions', of a song for record release and dance
purposes as early as the late 1960s (in some cases these mixes were
created for specific DJs). At the same time DJs developed a
style of presentation in which they would 'talkover' the sound of
the records to the audience (also called 'toasting'); as they began
to experiment with this form, adding reverb and special effects to
their performances, a new version, the 'dub' – a mix which eventually contained only the bare dance rhythms and bass line of the
original recording – was developed specifically for the purposes of
'toasting'.

While they are seldom described as such, the particular uses of
sound reproduction technology in reggae are, I think, fundamentally 'postmodern' in character. 'Postmodern' because they reflect,
firstly, a flexible attitude towards the recorded product (an object

that has previously been regarded, for the most part, as a fixed commodity form – static in its very nature) that is entirely new in popular culture. This is not simply of aesthetic significance but can equally be thought of as a form of empowerment: Dick Hebdige has referred to the practice of versioning as 'a democratic principle because it implies that no one has the final say. Everybody has a chance to make a contribution. And no one's version is treated as Holy Writ' (1987, 14). The practice of multiple mixes has since been taken up within the mainstream industry itself and become routine in dance music, resulting in a new kind of recording – the 'remix' record (I will return to this phenomenon later).

Secondly, the mixing of recorded and live elements characteristic of the 'talkover' represents a new level of integration of sound reproduction technology in popular music-making and a blurring of former distinctions between production and consumption. The rise of 'mediated-and-live' (Keil 1984) performance practices has become increasingly prevalent in a wide variety of musical styles – from Hip Hop and rap music to the *karaoke* bars of Japan – and perhaps needs to be considered as a new kind of 'humanizing or, better still, personalization of mechanical processes' (ibid., 94) in the postmodern era.

The international popularity of reggae is perhaps also a post-modern phenomenon in the sense that even before it was taken up within mainstream pop, the music had already gained a small international distribution through the circulation of records to communities of Jamaicans living on several continents. The reggae disco – the 'sound system' – became, in a sense, a technology and a cultural form designed to hold together this widely dispersed community – a force contributing to the construction of a 'deterritorialized "nationality"' (Guattari 1989) among Jamaicans throughout the world. It was only after this had been accomplished that reggae began to influence mainstream popular music.

A more general interaction between non-Western musics and Western pop (in both mediated and more direct forms) has been evident at least since the mid-1960s when Beatle George Harrison took up the sitar. But increasingly since the 1970s these influences have been multilateral, with pop musicians such as the Talking Heads, Kate Bush and Peter Gabriel tapping into a variety of musical traditions, on the one hand, and African and other popular musicians (such as King Sonny Ade of Nigeria) touring throughout the West, on the other. But one of the more interesting aspects of this general phenomenon for my purposes here is the technical base upon which the more recent exchanges are made: the role which samplers, multi-track recording technology, and sound reproduction more generally, play in making the exchange possible in the first place.

Paul Simon's *Graceland* album for example, released in 1986 (Warner Bros., 9254471), is a curious mix of American rock 'n' roll, country music, South African pop and Cajun Zydeco; rock 'n' roll is, in fact, a common denominator between all of these musical styles (the album itself became immensely popular despite criticism of Simon, on political grounds, for, among other things, violating a ban on working in South Africa). As Paul Simon relates in the album's liner notes, the musical inspiration for the album came after having only heard a cassette tape of South African jive; likewise, some of the songs were co-written with South African singer Joseph Shabalala after an exchange of cassette demo tapes. On any given song one finds that various vocal and instrumental tracks were laid in New York, or perhaps Johannesburg or London, others still in Los Angeles or Crowley, Louisiana. An album like *Graceland* would be virtually inconceivable at any other time in history: its musical foundation is the result of years of South African acculturation through mass media – South African pop sounding 'vaguely like '50s rock 'n' roll . . . familiar and foreign-sounding at the same time' (Paul Simon, album notes) – and the recording project technically impossible to co-ordinate and execute prior to the diffusion of multi-track recording equipment.

Listening to *Graceland* reminds me of Fredric Jameson's (1984) concern with 'surfaces' in postmodern aesthetics, his notions of 'schizophrenia' and 'hyperspace' (closed, self-sufficient spaces without perspective); the difference in the case of *Graceland* however is that one is perhaps likely to find these experiences more immediately pleasurable than Jamesons's feelings of disorientation and vertigo. In its sensibility, *Graceland* is a bit like a package tour: it skims across the surfaces of geography, history, ethnic and stylistic diversity. There is no particular understanding or commitment here, neither musical nor political (Simon has more recently shifted his attention to South America for his musical inspiration); one simply indulges in a series of fleeting musical moments, each strangely 'familiar and foreign-sounding at the same time'. Technically, such experiences are facilitated by a global system of music distribution, jet-age travel, and a sophisticated recording apparatus that allows diverse musical inputs from musicians in a variety of places and times to be synchronised, layered, manipulated and enhanced according to a single set of technical procedures.

Samplers and digital recording systems have only made sonic tours of exotic places easier, if somewhat more technically complex. For example, basic percussion parts on The Rolling Stones' song 'Continental Drift' were first programmed on a computer; later, Mick Jagger and his technician/keyboardist Matt Clifford travelled to Tangiers and made digital recordings of a Moroccan tribe and layered these onto the original parts; back in London, they over-dubbed yet another African group (this time from Upper Volta) who happened to the playing there at the time in a festival of 'world music'.

These examples, and countless others like them, may represent one aspect of a more general evolution in popular music described by Wallis and Malm: in their book they use the terms 'transculture' and 'transculturation' to describe the effects of the spread of technology and transnational production and marketing on popular music (1984: 300–11). Transcultural music is a form of music which has no clear origin within any particular ethnic group. In this sense, *Graceland* is transcultural music.

Random access and the 'technological imagination'

While I think Wallis and Malm's theoretical framework of the transcultural is useful in understanding specific cultural productions such as Paul Simon's *Graceland* I would like to situate this phenomenon within a more general framework that brings together similar practices and aesthetic attitudes that relate to a whole range of postmodern practices and discourses. In recent years a number of different technologies – including the binary digit of computer technology, television, data banks, communications networks and information systems – have been singled out and given special status as both symptom and metaphor for the postmodern condition as a whole (e.g. see Baudrillard 1983, Huyssen 1986, Jameson 1984, Lyotard 1984, Mowitt 1987). I will also privilege digital technology in this way by selecting a somewhat different metaphor: 'Random Access' – a technical term that relates to a configuration of memory storage in which any bit of information can, in theory, be accessed as rapidly as any other. The metaphor has the advantage of describing a state – a state of unheard of information densities, spatial compression, and a sense of temporal immediacy where nanoseconds (billionths of a second) become almost palpable – and a technical/cultural process where all musical expression becomes equally valid (and equally exploitable) by virtue of its accessibility.

To describe the postmodern condition of music in this way is not a form of poetry bordering on the hyperbolic; rather, it is based on real material conditions operating within musical culture today. For decades record producers (like Paul Simon) have regularly incorporated contributions from players located in different cities or countries – the various players need never meet one another; musicians who use samplers may choose their material from CD-ROM libraries containing literally thousands of sounds on a single disk or transmit sound data from one studio to another via telephone lines; computer-based sequencers (tape recorder-like programs) allow musicians to manipulate material with the precision of up to a 1/1920th note (ironically, they often do so in order to achieve the elusive 'feel' of live playing); viewers watch live concerts on television via satellite broadcasts; and with the Sony 'Walkman' listeners experience a continuous process in which sounds are combined with different contexts, a constantly shifting relationship between aural and visual space (see Hosokawa 1984).

'Random Access' is also the title of a sound sculpture created in 1963 by visual artist Nam June Paik: the work consists of several phonograph turntables with their tone arms detached; mounted on each turntable are rods which allow several records to spin simultaneously; the gallery visitors are invited to hold the tone arms in their hands and play any of the records (or several simultaneously) at will (John Cage's '33 1/3' and 'Twelve Radios' are works of a similar nature). In this sense, I have not selected this metaphor in order to single out the development of computers, per se, as the technical, economic or cultural event that serves as a signpost with which to mark the beginning of the postmodern era; on the contrary, as I have argued above, a number of technical developments since the late 1940s and early 1950s – including magnetic tape recording, LPs, television, transistor radios, cassettes *and* computers – have laid the basis for broad-based changes in social and cultural life during the decades that followed.

Of course, digital technologies have facilitated and extended the phenomenon of transculturation and what I would like to refer to here as 'random access culture'. As mentioned in passing above, the past decade has witnessed the growth of so-called 'sound libraries' for digital synthesisers, samplers and drum machines: each instrument comes with a collection (often numbering in the hundreds) of relatively standard instrument sounds – pianos, basses, saxophones, drums, brass and strings – in its memory banks; on most models, additional sounds can be obtained on cartridges, cards, diskettes or CD-ROMS and added to this basic repertoire. The sounds are usually tailored for specific styles of music and a small cottage industry has developed in order to maintain a steady supply of new sounds to keep up with changing tastes and musical styles. In many ways, high-tech music production has become something akin to a consumer practice where musicians are increasingly engaged in an exercise in consumer choice – choosing the right sounds for a given musical context or layering and combining several sounds to achieve a single instrumental effect (Théberge 1990). As in other areas of consumer culture, more is always better, and musicians' magazines in the 1980s were filled with descriptions of recording sessions where, for example, a rap musician might layer four bass drums from different drum machines or from sampled records in order to create a single kick drum part. Such practices are based on the assumption of a virtually unlimited access to sound material.

Along with the standard repertoire of sounds, it has also become commonplace for digital instruments to include a set of musical instrument and percussion sounds from different parts of the world (often simply labelled generically as 'ethnic' sounds). And not unlike the mass-produced objects found in import stores in almost any urban centre today, these sounds are marketed with the manufacturer's guarantee that no effort was spared in obtaining only the finest sounds from around the world, thus authenticating their origins (for those, unlike Paul Simon or Mick Jagger, who cannot afford to travel, import stores and sound libraries are the only viable alternative). The ubiquitous sound of the shakuhachi (a Japanese bamboo flute) in television advertising, films and popular music during the 1980s is an example of the shifting musical contexts in which sampled instrument sounds can be found; and it goes without saying that few of these contexts or the manner in which the sounds are played have anything to do with the cultural context or the musical stylistic traits appropriate to the instruments. Transcultural music-making demands that any instrument sound should be as available as any other; technological reproduction guarantees that availability and, in so doing, contributes to the increasing commodification of culture.

The growth of sound libraries, and the cottage industry that produces them, are a manifestation of two important aspects of digital musical instrument design. Firstly, they are a sign of the essential nature of these new technologies: digital synthesisers, samplers and drum machines are hybrid production/reproduction devices (see Oswald 1986); that is, to 'play' one of these instruments is also to 'playback' pre-recorded sounds and sequences of sounds.

In a certain sense, this puts the digital musical instrument industry in the same position as the gramophone industry at the turn of the century: just as one could not sell gramophones without also producing and selling records, one cannot now sell digital musical instruments without also producing and selling pre-fabricated sounds. Many manufacturers of digital instruments recognise that the production of sounds has become essential to the marketing of their products – software sells hardware – and, as a result, have shifted the responsibility for the production of sounds out of the hands of hardware designers and into the hands of their marketing departments or to outside specialists.

Secondly, and partly as a result of such moves, the production and marketing of sound programs has extended capitalist relations deeper into musical production and in this sense constitutes a new level of industrialisation and commodification within the music industry as a whole. Not unlike record producers, sound designers must try to understand musical trends and fashions so as to create the kinds of sounds that musicians will buy (indeed, hit record producers have been hired to create samples and sound programs by some manufacturers). The nature of this second-order entrepreneurial activity is entirely in keeping with organisational characteristics of the music industry since the mid-1950s as described by Peterson and Berger (1971): rapid changes in technology and market conditions created a 'turbulent' environment incompatible with traditional bureaucratic forms of organisation; the music industry responded by shifting the burden of production to outside entrepreneurs and concentrated on promotion, manufacturing and distribution. Such strategies are also characteristic of David Harvey's (1989) description of the deepening of capitalist relations and recent modes of 'flexible accumulation' in postmodern capitalist enterprise.

Of course, digital musical instruments, especially samplers, make use not only of instrument sounds but of *any* sound that can be recorded (even drum machines often include a number of sound effects – breaking glass, gun shots, screeching tyres – as part of their memory banks). In this sense, the commodification of sound is perhaps the logical extension of the modernist desire to make use of all possible sound phenomena in musical composition. First expressed by the Italian Futurist Luigi Russolo, and then taken up later by Edgard Varèse and the *musique concrète* school of composition in France of the 1950s, the desire to control and regulate natural sounds for musical purposes was an almost literal expression of the scientific philosophy of 'domination of nature' and of the subjection of the entire natural world to the order of production which is characteristic of modern instrumental reason.

In some ways, popular uses of samplers today exhibit a certain continuity with these modernist ideals and may be an example of the absorption of modernism into popular culture that has been cited by many as a characteristic of the postmodern era. Certainly, groups like the The Art of Noise (who took their name from the title of Russolo's manifesto of 1913) have taken up modernist techniques and processed them through a pop aesthetic; their music has even been described as something approaching *musique concrète* with a beat. But a major component of the modernist aesthetic of *musique concrète* composers, such as Pierre Schaeffer, was the manipulation of natural sound in order to render it abstract: Schaeffer's notion of the *objet sonore* is a conceptual, technical and quasi-scientific programme for the objectification of sound materials in order to render them more useful as abstract elements of art.

Much pop music, on the other hand, has tended to retain the sense of identity that sounds carry with them – their ability to act as a kind of referent for the object which is the source of the sound – thus leading to an aesthetic fundamentally based in collage and ironic juxtaposition. Furthermore, the tendency in pop to draw its sound materials from other media texts represents a predilection for that which is already cultural over that which is natural.

In this regard, recent technologies change our relationship not only to the world but also to the past, to our sense of social and cultural history. During the 1980s, many pop musicians (especially in dance genres such as Hip Hop) made use of samplers to collage together bits and pieces of rock, soul and funk records from the 1960s and 1970s. Some of the samples were recognisable, others not: samples of single drum sounds that could then be programmed into new rhythmic patterns or entire segments of a rhythmic groove (the 'beats' or 'breaks'), electric basses, guitars or James Brown's vocal pyrotechnics. Pop acts like M/A/R/R/S, Bomb The Bass, and others leaned towards the recognisable, adding snatches of cartoon music, radio broadcasts, classical music recordings and the like; and Canadian John Oswald's 'Plunderphonics' recordings made use of entire pop songs (referring to them as 'macrosamples') and subjected them to various treatments and manipulations – here again, mass recognition of the quoted material was essential. Strangely, the most technically innovative forms of pop music in the 1980s had become obsessed with self-referentiality, with the reproduction of pop culture's past (Goodwin 1988).

These practices can be regarded variously as a form of paying tribute (Hebdige 1987) or a form of irony. But in the case of some Hip Hop I think there is also a kind of ritual transferral of power where one takes technical control of sounds which themselves have, in the past, exerted a certain powerful effect on the individual. Again, these practices are not confined to musical materials alone: Hip Hoppers and rappers have sampled recordings of the voices of past Black leaders, such as Martin Luther King and Malcom X, and mixed them in with their rhythmic grooves. By attempting in this way to make a connection with a past from which they have been physically, and most often violently severed, rappers use sampling as a form of political practice and empowerment.

What is essential about all these practices however is that, firstly, they operate entirely within the realm of electronic reproducibility (these are not 'cover' versions of a song but uses of the actual recordings themselves); and secondly, they reflect a particular type of memory and subjectivity – a form of 'technological imagination' (Huyssen 1986: 9–10) that is the result of the experience of technology and everyday life within the matrix of mass media.

Baudrillard (1983), Jameson (1984) and Huyssen (1986) have all pointed, in different ways, to the media environment and its role in the collapse of a sense of historical time as an essential characteristic of postmodern culture. Similarly, Jonathan Crane (1986) has singled out Top 40 radio (a programme format first established in the USA during the 1950s that is characterised by the repetition of a limited number of songs derived from weekly trade magazine listings of top-selling records) for its particular configuration of media texts: through constant repetition, Top 40 radio ensures that our listening experience takes place in a state of constant recontextualisation, fostering a sense of 'interpretive instability', multiple readings and an endless awareness of the present (listening to tapes on a 'Walkman' can have similar effects). Crane argues that despite the media rhetoric of 'Golden Oldies', the airing of past hits ultimately makes us even more aware of our affective place in the present: even recent covers of old pop hits do not place us in the past, but rather, 'They operate by pretending to mimic older material while technologically recontextualizing the past in the present' (ibid., 68).

Sampling from old records and media texts, Top 40 radio formats, covers, and even industry profit strategies that led to CD reissues of old recordings (classical, jazz and pop) during the 1980s, are all different facets of an overall sonic environment that emphasises the present while giving an unprecedented access to the music of the past. The obsessive concentration on the present has been cited by Jameson (1984) as the hallmark of a schizophrenic subjectivity – a form of subjectivity which he, and others such as Crane and Harvey, take to be emblematic of the postmodern experience.

These characteristics are not confined to the world of popular culture alone. Certainly elements of collage, intertextuality and a sense of fragmented subjectivity have been commonplace in the work of a number of experimental artists since the early 1960s: Robert Ashley's multimedia and video 'operas' might be a good example. One of the most interesting works for my purposes here however is the third section of Luciano Berio's *Sinfonia* (1968, recorded on Columbia Records, MS 7268) – interesting, firstly, because it does not make use of electronic media (although Berio was no stranger to electronic music, the work is scored only for symphony orchestra and eight voices) and secondly, because it is the centrepiece of what might otherwise be considered a 'modernist' work. The third section of *Sinfonia* uses the third movement of Mahler's Second Symphony as a 'container' within which a large number of references to other music of the past and present are made; overlaid with this is a sprinkling of spoken and sung texts drawn from the work of Samuel Beckett and a wide range of other literary, popular and found texts. During the first two sections of *Sinfonia* there seems to be little doubt that one is listening to a 'serious' work: the apparent rigour of its tonal and formal structures seem to inform us of this fact and guarantee its existence as an autonomous work of modernist 'art'. But once the third section begins, the work opens up, loses its autonomy and its 'aura' (its distance, its unapproachability) completely and becomes, in a sense, invaded by the music of the past and present and the sounds of everyday life.

When this transformation takes place one is immediately struck by a number of radical shifts: the feeling of a fluctuating, multiple temporality; a difference in the perceived relationship between past and present; the nature of one's own subject position as listener; and the apparent dispersal of the unified subject, or persona, of the composer embodied in the work itself. All this adds up, despite the traditional character of the medium, to be the mark of a 'techno-logical imagination': the artistic practices of collage, assemblage and montage, used here in such a way as virtually to destroy the organic integrity of 'the work', are not unlike the strategies of various avant-garde movements described by Andreas Huyssen (1986; Huyssen makes a clear distinction between the avant-garde and modernism as such) and his assertion that they are the result of the transformation of everyday life by the technologies of mass production and reproduction.

Equally interesting are the texts chosen by Berio to accompany the music: they are characterised by the same incressant hyper-activity as the music, exhibit an excessive self-referentiality, directly address the audience and, perhaps most important, make both an implicit and an explicit attack on the notion of 'progress' – one of the key tenets of modernism and modernist art-making. 'Progress' here takes the form of the irrational call to 'keep going' when everything is in chaos and out of any apparent control.

It was Adorno who first asserted that the complete break with musical tradition, the realisation of a totalising formal organisation in music (which for Adorno was the equivalent of the musical 'domination of nature'; 1973, 64–7), the simultaneous liquidation and reassertion of the composer as 'subject', and the achievement of the absolute autonomy of the work represented 'progress' in the music of Arnold Schoenberg, a key modernist composer of the first half of this century. But it was the composer Edgard Varèse who, at about the same time, made an explicit link between the notion of musical 'progress' and the development of scientific knowledge and technological means. These two ideologies – total control and musical progress through technology – found their most powerful expression in the hyper-rational serialist school of *elektronische Musik* at Cologne during the early 1950s: from the outset, electronic music in Germany was regarded by its proponents as the fulfillment of a compositional ideal, 'the focal point of a progressive development' (Eimert 1958, 1); they realised that 'Only in coming to electronic music can one talk of real musical control of Nature' (ibid., 20).

The Cologne school applied Schoenberg's principles of organisation of pitch materials to all aspects of sound phenomena but it was in the control of timbre that they made their greatest strides. The control of timbre was decisive, firstly, because electronic sounds were thought to be free of external associations that would divert the attention of the listener away from the work itself. Secondly, and more importantly, for the first time the composer would be able to shape the microstructure of individual sounds in accordance with the overall compositional scheme – 'one comprehensive idea of working suffices to provide the elementary microstructure as well as the macrostructure of a composition' (Stockhausen 1958:51) – thus achieving an unprecedented unity in the formal structure of the work. By comparison, Schoenberg's music now appeared to be 'impure' because of the supposed 'contradiction' between his compositional ideas and the instrumental timbres that he was forced to use (Stockhausen 1961, 59).

Everything was done to ensure the uniqueness and integrity of the work: the technical plan and even the tapes containing the original timbres created for any individual work were destroyed after the composition had been realised; no two works would be allowed to have structural similarities that would identify them as part of a 'tradition'. And more to the point, the absolute uniqueness of the work functioned ideologically as an implicit critique of commodification and mass reproduction in the capitalist culture industry. In this sense, the high modernism of 1950s serialism was a clear expression of what Huyssen (1986) has called the 'great divide' that separated modernism from mass culture.

It would be naive to ignore the continuing power of the ideology of 'progress' in the legitimation of scientific knowledge and technological development during the postmodern era. And I would certainly not wish to argue that new digital music technologies (in both pop and 'serious' music) do not continue to make a fetish out of the idea of total control (even if the extreme aesthetics of serialism no longer operate). But nevertheless, it is curious to observe the degree to which technology put in the service of modernist, instrumental reason differs from the aesthetics of the 'technological imagination': the technological imagination – the 'random access' aesthetic characteristic of electronic reproduction – welcomes the confusion caused by outside associations; works to enhance the differences found in its materials rather than homogenising them into an abstract form of total unity; and, in its reworking of musical traditions and mass media sounds and images, implicates itself in the commodity culture around it rather than seeking the refuge of artistic autonomy.

Electronic (re)production

The worlds of mass media and electronic reproduction have been key elements in the arguments presented thus far but it still remains to be demonstrated whether electronic reproduction differs in any fundamental way from mechanical reproduction in the earlier part of this century. In 1936, when Walter Benjamin wrote his now famous essay 'The Work of Art in the Age of Mechanical Reproduction' (1969) he could still write confidently about the shock effect of film montage, about musical performances and their mechanical reproduction, about originals and copies. There was a sense in which reproduction could still be juxtaposed against some referent, some notion of reality (albeit a reality whose 'aura' was shrinking).

But music production in the postmodern era does not permit one to speak with such confidence: mainstream techniques of editing magnetic tape in music production have been, from the outset, more subtle than those of film and instead of producing 'shock', these techniques achieve a seamlessness that leaves most listeners unaware of the constructed nature of the recorded music they listen to. By the mid 1980s, many performances of contemporary popular music could hardly sustain the notion of a 'live' event – they had become hybrid events making use of much prerecorded material in order to achieve their goal of being as faithful as possible to the recorded product. And ever since the adoption of multi-track recording equipment during the 1960s, recordings had no longer been tied to any pre-existing musical event – the product of a variety of musical contributions recorded at different times and places, the multi-track recording is a 'simulacrum' (Baudrillard 1983) in the fullest sense of the term: the perfect copy for which there exists no original.

The idea of the recording as simulacrum can be thought of in other ways as well and in order to illustrate this I want to look at the relationship between recording practices and acoustic space (see also Théberge 1989). In what might be considered a 'modernist', or perhaps 'realist', aesthetic of recording prevalent throughout the early half of this century, engineers worked under the banner of 'high fidelity' while searching for ever more powerful means with which to reproduce the sound of musical instruments and concert hall acoustics. Their aim was to reproduce the 'aura' of the concert hall experience – the acoustic conditions that helped to construct the 'unique phenomenon of a distance' which Benjamin argued was characteristic of ritual and 'auratic' experience. But with the arrival of electronic technologies the recording medium slowly became *productive* of the real, not merely reproductive.

This occurred as engineers tried to gain greater control over the recording environment, first through novel microphone placements, and later through modifications of studio architecture (the dampening of naturally-occurring acoustic reflections) and the use of artificial reverberation devices. Over the years the list of devices used in order to simulate natural room reverberation have included acoustic chambers (small rooms isolated from the main recording area), mechanical reverbs (springs and plates), and electronic and digital delays. The degree to which we have become accustomed to (or have grown to prefer) the sound of artificial reverberation is implied in the fact that most digital effects devices today include settings that attempt to recreate not only natural acoustics but also the sound of room and plate reverbs of the past – with digital technology we have entered an era of second-order simulation.

In multi-track recording it has become standard practice to add different types and different amounts of artificial reverberation to each voice or instrument after it has been recorded (many synthesisers, drum machines and samplers even include reverberation as part of the basic make-up of individual sound programs). In the final mix, the resulting sound consists of a set of multiple, fragmented acoustic spaces that is completely artificial in character. This 'simulacrum' of acoustic space could also be described in Jameson's terms as a kind of 'hyperspace' (mentioned earlier in conjunction with the global, ethnic/geographic configuration of transcultural recording projects). Here the idea of 'hyperspace' could be thought to operate at the level of the sonic environments created within, and by, the recording itself.

The mastery over the spatial aspects of sound in popular music recording practice (including not only control of reverberant information, as I have described here, but also the use of microphones and the panning of sounds in the final, stereo mix) is not unlike the kind of technical control that modernist composers of *musique concrète* and *elektronische Musik* had attempted to establish over the spatial aspects of their work during the 1950s. Composers such as Karlheinz Stockhausen began to think of the performance environment as an extension of the work itself and sought to give each composition its own, unique spatial organisation and projection. In this way, one of the goals of high modernism became the integration of the micro-level of the tonal structure, the macro-level of the work, and the meta-level of the performance space within a single formal plan.

But the 'hyperspace' created by pop recording practices differs from this modernist strategy because it is obviously due, in part, to the nature of the recording environment: the multi-track recording studio is a non-space – a space that has been rendered acoustically neutral by sound absorbing materials (those huge, mythic snare drum sounds that are characteristic of so many pop records are made, initially, in a space not much larger, and with considerably less acoustic resonance, than a closet). In the parlance of recording engineers, the acoustics of the average pop studio are 'dead'. Reverb is added to the recording, in part, to counter the effect on sounds made in such an unusually 'dead' space.

I say 'in part', because the sounds of pop music do not adhere to any pre-existing notions of 'the work' or of acoustic realism (there is no pop equivalent to the classical music concert hall); but rather, they are tailored to fill the equally 'dead' spaces of suburban living rooms and motor car interiors. Pop sounds the way it does because it is designed for a particular pattern of *consumption* (not simply because of the exigencies of production or because of an exclusive focus on the formal integrity of the art object). And in this sense, Benjamin's dictum still holds true: 'To an ever greater degree the work of art reproduced becomes the work of art designed for reproducibility' (1968, 224); modes of production and consumption are intimately tied in the age of electronic media.

'Dead' space is transformed by pop recordings into a 'hyper-space' of seemingly boundless, mythic proportions. During the summer months, when one hears the sound of pop music spilling out from the rolled-down windows of passing cars, one can gain an impression of the power that is being invested in those mobile interiors. The driver not only enjoys the power of driving a machine (which Baudrillard claims is no longer a true form of pleasure; 1983, 127) but also revels in the 'hyperspace' created by the pop recording. This 'hyperspace', and the uncommon closeness with which the microphone reveals and amplifies every sensuous detail of musical sound, endows domestic space with a degree of intensity which may act as a kind of postmodern surrogate for the absence of more genuinely ritualised or 'auratic' experiences. But there is nothing inherent in this experience that leads, necessarily, to the type of political consciousness that Benjamin had hoped for: the power invested in these technologically enhanced spaces is all simulation and seduction.

Multi-track recording practices have also called into question the idea of the 'original', or 'master' recording. The aesthetic and economic implications of this tendency have been most clearly explored in the field of dance music. During the 1970s and 1980s innovative producers and engineers with a keen entrepreneurial sense of the needs of a variety of markets realised that multi-track technology (and later, samplers) allowed them to tailor mixes for different applications – an album mix, a radio mix, an extended dance club mix, etc.; any one of these might then be taken up by DJs or other producers and mixed into further variations. Such practices make the notion of a single, definitive 'original' irrelevant.

In economic terms, multiple mixes can be considered as part of a more general set of strategies that David Harvey (1989) has referred to as 'flexible capital accumulation' in postmodern industry:

> Remixing a song reactivates it in the cultural marketplace. As the trade and popular press have reported, the remix version of a song is treated as a *different* version, generating additional revenue without the need for a new melody or lyrics. (Tankel 1990, 41)

Music production in the postmodern period then is characterised by an increasing erosion in the status of the real – the live performance as originating event and the acoustic resonance of actual space – and even the notion of a single, original mould from which 'copies' are made.

With the new technical potential available to them producers and engineers have taken an increasingly active role in the construction of the musical product, thus blurring former distinctions between composer and producer, musician and technician. The erosion of the status of the real has thus been accompanied by a breakdown in the notion of authorship:

> the Van Meegeren syndrome can no longer be cited as an indictment but becomes rather an entirely appropriate description of the aesthetic condition of our time. The role of the forger, of the unknown maker of unauthenticated goods, is emblematic of electronic culture.
>
> (Gould 1966, 56)

Shortly after Glenn Gould unceremoniously departed from the concert stage in 1964 in order to explore fully the possibilities offered by the recording studio, he claimed Hans van Meegeren, a forger of Vermeer paintings, as one of his 'private heroes'. Gould used the van Meegeren story as a kind of modern parable representing the crisis of authorship that was inherent in electronic media practices (where the roles of composer, producer, musician and engineer merge in unpredictable ways) and the resulting erosion in the authority of the critic, who could no longer judge the authenticity of the work of art through mere observation. Not surprisingly, Gould was thereafter regularly chastised by critics for his recordings with their highly edited performances, their 'distortions' and 'excesses' that were so uncharacteristic of the tradition of concert hall performance.

In 1964 Rob Pilatus and Fab Morvan, front men for the pop group Milli Vanilli, had not yet been born but some twenty-six years later they would become the centre of a controversy illustrating that Gould's notion of the forger was indeed 'emblematic' of what had by then come to be known as the 'postmodern' era. In 1989 the group's first album, *Girl You Know It's True,* won the duo a Grammy award for Best New Artist; by 1990 the album had sold over ten million copies. No small part of this success had been due to the hip, high-fashion image and the dynamic dance moves of the two performers in live concerts and, especially, in music videos. But when it was revealed that neither performer had ever sung a single note on their recording, the National Academy of Recording Arts and Sciences withdrew their award (ironically, the scandal had erupted after an argument between the duo and their producer, Frank Farian, in which the two performers demanded that they actually be allowed to sing on their next album). The action taken by NARAS was predictable: those who had legitimised the group's success had to be the first to disown them. But what made this incident interesting was the fact that the speed with which the media outcry and the accusations of fraud ended was even greater than the velocity with which the group had ascended to MTV fame. While the public seemed bemused by the incident, few expressed outright shock. Indeed, it appeared that for many people the 'controversy' was a non-event: the pertinent question arising from the group's demise was not so much 'What's real?' as 'who cares?'.

On the surface, the Milli Vanilli incident might appear insignificant, a sensational exception to the rule (although the press was quick to point out that questions concerning the authenticity of recordings by a variety of pop acts have been raised periodically ever since the 1960s). Surely, Pilatus's and Morvan's careers in the music business ended the day their 'secret' was revealed. But producer Frank Farian, and others like him, will no doubt continue to make recordings because their role is central to the technological apparatus that made Milli Vanilli possible in the first place. In the final analysis neither Milli Vanilli nor fraud were the issue – the issue was technology.

For months prior to the Milli Vanilli fiasco media critics had expressed concern with a trend towards the use of digital samplers and prerecorded backing tapes to replace vocals in performances by a variety of pop performers. Several state legislatures in the USA had even begun drafting bills that would require concert tickets to inform consumers if a concert was not entirely 'live' (once again however, it was unclear whether fans themselves were particularly concerned about the practice of lip-syncing in performance). For the critics and legislators, the problem was not simply that musicians were trying to sound like their recordings when performing on stage (this had long been a preoccupation among pop musicians), but that concerts had indeed *become* recordings (Handelman 1990, 15).

It is interesting to note that the fuss concerning the Milli Vanilli 'fraud' was mainly focused on the vocal portion of live performances: the voice, it would seem, is too personal, too intimate, too bound up with Romantic notions of individual identity, creativity and authenticity to be allowed to be reproduced in 'live' contexts. The reproduction of other instruments – strings, horns and, more recently, even bass and drums – has become something of a norm in concert performances ever since the introduction of digital synthesisers and samplers. Even the Rolling Stones, arguably one of the most 'authentic' rock acts of the past three decades, used synthesisers and samplers on their 'Steel Wheels' tour of 1989/90 in order to reproduce, 'live', the horns, strings, acoustic guitars and other sounds from their hit records of the 1960s. With digital samplers, even the distinction between 'live' and 'recorded' instruments has become blurred: the Pet Shop Boys have stated that they prefer to use samplers and sequencers on stage rather than backing tapes because they *sound* more 'live' than recorded instruments (even though, technically speaking, sampled sounds are 'recorded' sounds they have the feel of being 'played' by the computer during performance; Pet Shop Boys tour brochure 1989).

But the issue of the 'live' versus the 'recorded' aside, perhaps what was really at stake in the Milli Vanilli scandal was the fact that the voice of the pop star – which is one of the focal points of identification between the star and the consumer – is the music industry's most essential commodity: by compromising the authentic status of the voice the entire enterprise, or so it would seem, had been put at risk.

In this regard, the career of avant-garde performance artist/pop star Laurie Anderson is particularly intriguing because she has made the voice the site of a number of technological transgressions.

The audience's access to her – their ability to identify with her – as a star is constantly thwarted by an ironic distance created by the various devices – tape recorder tricks, Vocoders, harmonisers and delays – that she employs in order to alter, distort and multiply her vocal persona. Indeed, for Anderson, it would seem that verbal communication, and even the notion of an 'authentic' voice, is made problematic by technology:

> (Examples of paranormal voices on tape.
> What are paranormal voices on tape?
> They are voices of unknown origin.
> They are paranormal voices on tape –)
> (lyric from 'Example #22', *Big Science*,
> Warner Bros. Records, XBS 3674)

From the outset, Laurie Anderson's work has been regarded by many writers as quintessentially 'postmodern': this status can been conferred on her for a variety of reasons including the feminist and deconstructivist aspects of her work, her involvement with mass culture (and her simultaneous critique of, and 'complicity' with, it), and her near-schizophrenic ability to adopt and project multiple subject positions (for discussions of Anderson's work in relation to postmodernism see Hutcheon 1989, Huyssen 1986, McClary 1991, Owens 1983, Pfeil 1988). But what interests me here is the way that these various aspects of Anderson's work have been articulated through her use of technology (a significant point in itself given the male domination of technological expertise in music) and, especially, her use of technology and the human voice.

An early example of Anderson's approach to the sound of the human voice involves a specially-designed violin that she made frequent use of during the late 1970s: where the bridge should have been, the violin was equipped with a tape recorder playback head; and instead of horse hair, the bow was strung with a prerecorded magnetic tape; a number of bows might be used in the course of a performance, several containing the sound of voices. Bowing the violin in a conventional fashion produced a variety of distortions in the vocal sound resulting from speed changes, backwards and forwards playback, truncated strokes, etc. The immediate effect of this technique was, firstly, to externalise the voice, to problematise the relationship between the voice and the body of the performer (the eroticisation of the voice/body equation is especially powerful with regard to female performers in popular music); and secondly, to transform it into a 'paranormal' voice – a mediated voice exhibiting varying degrees of intelligibility and deliberate distortion. The act of playing the violin also created an ambiguous relationship between performance and electronic reproduction: had Anderson used the violin to play the recording medium? or, perhaps, the recording medium to play the violin? – it was impossible to decide which was the more convincing description of the event.

Anderson has also regularly used harmonisers in order to shift the pitch of her voice down an octave, heightening the audience's perception of sexual difference. At the same time she appropriates the sound of the male voice, plays with it, transforms it from the voice of authority into the voice of the huckster or the TV personality. All this is done with a certain irony, a certain degree of vaudevillian flair. There is both a clear feminist intent and a deconstructivist mode of operation evident in such practices; furthermore, the manner in which Anderson combines avant-garde techniques, gender awareness and popular cultural forms is entirely postmodern in character.

In performance and in songs such as 'O Superman', Anderson creates little vignettes in which she might adopt several different voices – the individual character of each voice supported by some kind of technical distortion that identifies it. The succession of these voices is always swift, producing a sense of multiple, fragmented, constantly shifting and dissolving personae. The vignettes and the technical devices short-circuit any notion of vocal 'authenticity' – if Anderson is expressing herself then who is 'she'? – and simultaneously alter the conventional processes of audience identification.

At a more general level, Anderson makes use of two kinds of technology: makeshift devices constructed according to her own design (such as the violin/tape recorder described above); and a wide range of standard, off-the-shelf synthesisers, signal processors, tape recorders (including telephone answering machines) and other electronic instruments typically found in the worlds of popular music production and consumer culture. Her use of this latter group of instruments can be understood not only as a conscious turn towards the technologies of popular culture but also as an implicit break with the institutionalised facilities (and aesthetics) of 'serious' electronic music: along with Philip Glass and a number of other postmodern composers, Anderson began her career using inexpensive popular instruments – Farfisa organs, Casio consumer keyboards and the like – that were anathema to the high modernist tradition (as a rule, keyboard instruments were avoided by electronic composers of the 1950s and early 1960s because of their association with traditional forms of music).

Indeed, because of the costs and technical expertise involved, it could be argued that the early development of electronic and computer music – in state-run radio facilities, universities and corporate laboratories such as Bell Labs – had been a key moment in the institutionalisation of modernist music during the postwar period. The dream of an autonomous scientific research facility, unconstrained by social and commercial pressures and devoted to experimentation in music and acoustics, had been a central theme in the technological wing of modernist ideology from the time of Varèse. And in recent decades that dream has been largely realised at centres such as Stanford, MIT, and the Institute de Recherche et Coordination Acoustique/Musique in Paris. The research carried out at these centres is both a tribute to modernist ideology and an important source of its continuing legitimation in the face of the mass market forces that currently determine electronic musical instrument design.

While aesthetic orientation was doubtlessly the more important factor, the adoption of keyboard instruments developed for the popular market was certainly among the first concrete steps made by Anderson, Glass and others across the 'great divide' (Huyssen 1986) that separated modernism from mass culture. Since then, these composers have made an increasing use of popular modes of production (Glass's ensemble has for years included a full-time sound engineer, and his opera recordings make use of multi-track techniques rarely found in 'classical' music recordings) and have ventured into a number of collaborative recording projects with popular musicians. While I agree with Georgina Born (1987) that there is much that is misleading about the various collaborations/cross-overs of artists such as Philip Glass, David Byrne, Brian Eno and others, and that the art worlds of avant-garde postmodernists and popular musicians are, to a large extent, still separate, I would still argue that Laurie Anderson (as is evident stylistically in her most recent albums such as *Strange Angels*, Warner Bros. Records, 92 59001) has gone further than most in developing collaborative relationships (with musician Peter Gabriel, producer Nile Rodgers and others) that have significantly influenced the direction of her work.

Anderson's break with modernism goes deeper than her aesthetic orientation towards pop culture, however; much of her work (for example, the album *Big Science*) explicitly challenges the legitimacy of science and notions of technological 'progress'. Ironically, her work is completely dependent on technology and in this way she openly reveals her own complicity with it and with the structures of capitalism. Her ability to sustain the critique while acknowledging her complicity suggests that postmodernism *is* capable of going beyond the modernist strategies of total negation advocated by earlier culture critics such as Adorno.

Conclusion

Electronic technologies have become pervasive in our society (and indeed throughout the world) since the Second World War and have become not only one of the preconditions for musical culture but also a mediating factor in virtually all areas of social and cultural exchange. In this regard, Laurie Anderson's *uses* of technology must be seen as only a part of a much wider range of direct and indirect references and allusions to media and technology in her work as a whole. But the relationship between technology and artistic production is often much less direct (and certainly less obvious) than in the work of artists such as Anderson: indeed, a postmodern sensibility is not dependent on the use of specific technologies or techniques at all (and in this I disagree with certain writers, such as Andrew Goodwin 1988, who have attempted to define specific uses of technology narrowly as 'postmodern'); but rather, it is a 'structure of feeling' (Williams 1977, 125–8) that is in large part informed by the experience of technology in everyday life but is expressed in a variety of different (and sometimes contradictory) ways and in many different media (technological or otherwise).

I have attempted to describe some of the contours of this sensibility here and to relate it to specific developments in the history of sound technology and to patterns of organisation and distribution in the recording industries during the postwar period. The notion of 'Random Access' that I have suggested is, I think, a useful way of condensing certain aspects of the postmodern sensibility into a metaphorical expression that highlights their origins in the experience of technical media. In this, I have been influenced by a number of postmodern theorists and am especially indebted to Andreas Huyssen who has attempted to theorise the developments and transformations of postmodernism during the 1960s and 1970s:

> The situation in the 1970s seems to be characterized rather by an ever wider dispersal and dissemination of artistic practices all working out of the ruins of the modernist edifice, raiding it for ideas, plundering its vocabulary and supplementing it with randomly chosen images and motifs from pre-modern and non-modern cultures as well as from contemporary mass culture. Modernist styles have actually not been abolished, but, as one art critic recently observed, continue 'to enjoy a kind of half-life in mass culture' . . . Yet another way of putting it would be to say that all modernist and avantgardist techniques, forms and images are now stored for instant recall in the computerized memory banks of our culture. But the same memory also stores all of pre-modernist art as well as the genres, codes, and image worlds of popular cultures and modern mass culture. (Huyssen 1986, 196)

But unlike Huyssen I do not wish to imply that popular culture simply draws on modernist forms and techniques (e.g. in the ways characteristic of so much recent advertising and commercial design): the techniques employed in rap and other recent styles of popular music-making, while they may bear a resemblance to earlier modernist or avant-garde strategies, arise out of genuine responses to postmodernity as a general condition and from the perspective of specific social, racial and cultural vantage points both within and outside of it.

Secondly, in relation to earlier forms of mechanical reproduction, electronic technologies differ qualitatively in the manner in which they engage in the process of reproduction: indeed, in many ways they have become *productive* of 'the real' rather than merely reproductive. In popular music production, electronic technologies create a 'simulacrum' – a complete simulation of musical instrument sounds, performance practices and acoustic space; and in the sphere of consumption, electronic technologies are used to create a kind of 'hyperspace' – an altered relationship to the spatial/temporal experience of the acoustic and visual environment.

But in a very different way, the borderlines between production and consumption have become blurred through the uses of electronic technologies: in recording studios, the use of digital synthesisers, samplers and drum machines (with their libraries of prefabricated sound programs) is a process simultaneously of production and consumption; and outside the professional studios, the diverse uses of cassette tape recorders (originally developed as a consumer technology) have created a vibrant underground of independent musical production and distribution.

Throughout this discussion, I have tended to privilege production and consumption practices in popular culture and have ignored many intriguing uses of technology in 'art' music. I have done so, in part, because much postmodernist music still seems to be marginialized within the institutions of art music, where the conservative defence of the traditional canon continues almost unabated. Technical innovations in popular music, on the other hand, occur in the mainstream where they both influence, and respond to, the powers and pressures of media institutions.

But perhaps equally important, the high-tech fringe of art music – the computer music researcher and composer – tends to be still largely modernist in character, still concerned with notions of progress and exhibiting a hostile attitude towards mass culture and a lack of interest in the processes of musical reception by the audience. Even in what, to my mind, are some of its most eloquent expressions in theory and criticism (see, for example, Gaburo 1985), computer music displays a profoundly problematic relationship to music of the past and continues to valorise notions of a 'pure', creative relationship between humans and machines.

But again, popular music privileges no particular relationship to technology: indeed, the diversity of uses inherent in popular culture denies the possibility of any such strategy. In contemporary culture everything has been touched by technology, transformed and contaminated by it; and, almost as if in response to this fact, popular musicians and consumers use, adapt, 'scratch' and abuse technology for their own ends with little or no concern for abstract notions of the 'true' character of the technology or its intended purposes.

In this sense, electronic technologies have not only become the environment in which music is produced and consumed in the postmodern era, they have also become a medium through which significant aesthetic, social and cultural processes are activated and sustained.

References

Adorno, Theodor (1973), *The Philosophy of Modern Music*, trans. A. Mitchell and W. Blomster (New York).

Attali, Jacques (1977), *Bruits: essai sur l'économie politique de la musique*. Paris: Presses Universitaires de France.

Baudrillard, Jean (1983), 'The Ecstacy of Communication' in Hal Foster ed., *The Anti-Aesthetic*, (Port Townsend, Washington), pp. 126–34.

Benjamin, Walter (1969), 'The Work of Art in the Age of Mechanical Reproduction', in *Illuminations*, ed. Hannah Arendt, trans. H. Zohn (New York), pp. 217–51.

Born, Georgina (1987), 'Modern Music Culture: On Shock, Pop and Synthesis', *New Formations*, no. 2 (summer), pp. 51–78.

Crane, Jonathan (1986), 'Mainstream Music and the Masses', *Journal of Communication Inquiry*, vol. 10, no. 3, pp. 66–70.

Eimert, Herbert (1958), 'What is Electronic Music?', *Die Reihe*, no. 1, pp. 1–10.

Frith, Simon (1986), 'Art versus Technology: The Strange Case of Popular Music', *Media, Culture and Society*, vol. 8, no. 3, pp. 263–79.

Gaburo, Kenneth (1985), 'The Deterioration of an Ideal, Ideally Deteriorized: Reflections on Pietro Grossi's "Paganini A1 Computer"', *Computer Music Journal* vol. 9, no. 1 (summer), pp. 39–44.

Goodwin, Andrew (1988), 'Sample and Hold: Pop Music in the Digital Age of Reproduction', *Critical Quarterly*, vol. 30, no. 3 (autumn), pp. 34–49.

Gould, Glenn (1966), 'The Prospects of Recording', *High Fidelity*, no. 16 (April), pp. 46–63.

Guattari, Félix (1989), 'The Three Ecologies', *New Formations*, no. 8 (summer), pp. 131–48.

Handelman, David (1990), 'Is It Live Or . . .', *Rolling Stone*, no. 156 (6 Sept.), pp. 15–16.

Harvey, David (1989), *The Condition of Postmodernity* (Cambridge, Mass.).

Hebdige, Dick (1987), *Cut 'n' Mix* (London).

Hosokawa, Shuhei (1984), 'The Walkman Effect', *Popular Music*, no. 4, pp. 165–80.

Hutcheon, Linda (1989), *The Politics of Postmodernism* (London).

Huyssen, Andreas (1986), *After the Great Divide: Modernism, Mass Culture, Postmodernism* (Bloomington, Ind.).

Jameson, Fredric (1984), Postmodernism, or The Cultural Logic of Late Capitalism', *New Left Review*, no. 146, pp. 53–92.

Keil, Charles (1984), 'Music Mediated and Live in Japan', *Ethnomusicology*, vol. 28, no. 1, pp. 91–6.

Laing, Dave (1986), 'The Music Industry and the "Cultural Imperialism" Thesis', *Media, Culture and Society* vol. 8, no. 3, pp. 331–41.

Lyotard, Jean-François (1984), *The Postmodern Condition: A Report on Knowledge* (Minneapolis and Manchester).

McClary, Susan (1991), *Feminine Endings: Music, Gender, and Sexuality* (Minneapolis, Minn.).

Mowitt, John (1987), 'The Sound of Music in the Era of its Electronic Reproducibility." in R. Leppert and S. McClary ed., *Music and Society* (Cambridge), pp. 173–97.

Nettl, Bruno (1964), *Theory and Method in Ethnomusicology* (London).

Oswald, John (1986), 'Plunderphonics or, Audio Piracy as a Compositional Prerogative', *Musicworks*, no. 34 (spring), pp. 5–8.

Owens, Craig (1983), 'The Discourse of Others: Feminists and Postmodernism' in Hal Foster ed., *The Anti-Aesthetic* (Port Townsend, Washington), pp. 57–82.

Pareles, Jon (1987), 'Record-It-Yourself Music on Cassette', *The New York Times* (11 May), p. C13.

Peterson, Richard A. and Berger, David G. (1971), 'Entrepreneurship in Organizations: Evidence from the Popular Music Industry', *Administrative Quarterly*, no. 16, pp. 97–106.

Pfeil, Fred (1988), 'Postmodernism as a "Structure of Feeling"' in Lawrence Grossberg and Cary Nelson ed., *Marxism and the Interpretation of Culture* (Urbana, Ill.). pp. 381–403.

Regev, Motti (1986), 'The Soundscape as a Contest Area: "Oriental Music" and Israeli Popular Music', *Media, Culture and Society*, vol. 8, no. 3, pp. 343–55.

Stockhausen, Karlheinz (1958), 'Actualia', *Die Reihe*, no. 1, pp. 45–51.

Stockhausen, Karlheinz (1961) 'Two Lectures', *Die Reihe*, no. 5, pp. 59–82.

Tankel, Jonathan David (1990), 'The Practice of Recording Music: Remixing as Recoding', *Journal of Communication* vol. 40, no. 3 (summer), pp. 34–46.

Théberge, Paul (1989), 'The "Sound" of Music: Technological Rationalization and the Production of Popular Music', *New Formations*, no. 8 (summer), pp. 99–111.

Théberge, Paul (1990), 'Consumers of Technology: Musicians as Market', *ONETWOTHREEFOUR*, no. 9 (autumn), pp. 53–60.

Wallis, Roger and Malm, Krister (1984), *Big Sounds from Small Peoples* (New York).

Williams, Raymond (1977), *Marxism and Literature* (Oxford).

Index